May "I" always bring you blessings in return as you bless the food He brings as you create it for others with love
Mommy ♡

26/0
£5.00

Gluten-Free
GOES GOURMET

GLUTEN FREE · DAIRY FREE · CORN FREE
LOW GLYCEMIC · KOSHER

Gluten-Free
GOES GOURMET

VICKY PEARL

Typeset and designed by RachelAdlerDesign.com

ISBN-10: 1-885220-77-4
ISBN-13: 978-1-885220-77-6

Printed in Canada by PTEX Group,
www.ptexgroup.com

Distributed by:

Moznaim Publishing Co.

4304 12th Ave
Brooklyn, NY 11219-1301

Tel: (718) 438-7680

Fax: (718) 438-1305

www.moznaim.com

Acknowledgments

My heart overflows

with gratitude and thanks to G-d, who, in His infinite bounty, has enabled me to present this book to you.

Publishing this book, however, required nothing short of a small army of professionals and colleagues, as well as a devoted community of family and friends who kindly donated their time and energy, all of whom played a central role in its completion.

Most central, perhaps, was my brilliant and supportive editor, Daphna Rabinovitch, who, through the sheer magic of her professionalism, expertise, and overall kind nature, elevated this collection from merely good to what I only considered a dream. Thanks to her these recipes not only make sense but also answer every question you may think of. Every detail is considered, and the prose unnervingly reflects what I sometimes didn't even have words to say.

Many thanks are due to Chaya Baila Gavant, my proofreader. Her meticulous attention to detail coupled with her winning personality made her a pleasure to work with. The complete and reader-friendly index is a result of her keen talents.

I am grateful to the accomplished Rachel Adler, a graphic artist of the highest order. An upstanding individual, she endowed the book with a wonderful flow, a profound realism, and an overall sense of flair.

Ruchy Schon is, simply put, a photographer extraordinaire and one of the kindest people I've been lucky enough to meet. Her photographer's eye made the food that graces these pages come alive, adopt a personality all its own, and become a true hero.

I was blessed to have the creative duo Blimi Orliansky and Malkie Ryba share their amazing talents with me. With endless love, zest, and imagination, they did the food styling and props for every single photo so the recipes were authentically represented and the food as inspired as the dishes that held it.

To my clients, thank you for your encouragement and patience. You are what got me started in the first place. In your honor, a huge and varied population can now start to restore their health and rediscover the joy of cooking, despite the limitations of food sensitivities.

CONTENTS

Stellar Side Dishes

Beautiful Breads

Delightful Desserts

Creative Cakes & Cookies

Understanding The Healthy Way

I was very honored

to be asked to write the introduction for this wonderful cookbook. Having written a book myself and seen many hundreds of patients with gluten intolerance, I know the importance of having cookbooks that embrace healthy, gluten-free, dairy-free meals.

Gluten intolerance, an umbrella term that I use to include both celiac disease and gluten sensitivity, is extremely underdiagnosed in this country. Celiac disease is missed 95 percent of the time in the United States. It seems shocking, but the truth is that we only diagnose 5 percent of those suffering. For gluten sensitivity, the numbers are thought to be even higher.

Gluten is a protein found in wheat, rye, barley, and related grains such as spelt and kamut, to name a few. This protein is often not well digested in the human body, and is known to be responsible for creating over three hundred

conditions and diseases that literally touch every system and organ in the human body. From digestive problems to hormonal imbalances, from skin conditions to lung problems, and from liver disease to depression, the wide-reaching effects of gluten are too numerous to name.

Initially, it was thought that the protein could only cause digestive complaints, as that was where it resided after consumption. We have now come to realize that the partially digested protein fragments can leave the intestine via the bloodstream and create havoc throughout the body.

Unfortunately, many clinicians remain "stuck" in the early description of the disease and believe that if a patient isn't underweight or suffering from diarrhea and digestive pain, there is no reason to test her for gluten intolerance.

Nothing could be further from the truth, but old habits and beliefs can be difficult to change.

The facts are that gluten can cause inflammation in the brain, nervous system, and skin. As a response to gluten, the immune system creates antibodies to attack it because it sees it as a toxin. These antibodies can in turn mistakenly attack other organs in the body in a fashion that causes autoimmune diseases to develop. Interestingly, new research has revealed that while gluten creates problems throughout the body, the answer to the problem truly does reside in the health of the small intestine.

The probiotic population—or good bacteria—in the small intestine not only outnumbers cells in the body by ten times, but also has one hundred more genes than the human body. How is this significant? It is thought that these probiotics actually have the ability to keep bad genes turned off. In other words, if you were born with the genes that cause celiac disease but had a healthy probiotic population, this could prevent the celiac disease gene from being turned on.

While we have a long way to go to increase awareness of gluten intolerance, it is happening. Personally, I am committed to it and so is Vicky, the author of this cookbook. If you've already been diagnosed with celiac disease or gluten sensitivity, your goal needs to be restoring health to your digestive tract while studiously avoiding all gluten and any other foods that you react to. That begins with what you put in your mouth each and every meal.

You were wise to purchase this book, which is full of wonderful recipes that will keep you and your family healthy and satisfied while helping to restore your good health.

DR. VIKKI PETERSON, DC, CCN

FOUNDER OF HEALTHNOW MEDICAL CENTER

COAUTHOR OF *The Gluten Effect*

AUTHOR OF THE EBOOK *Gluten Intolerance: What You Don't Know May Be Killing You!*

Appreciating
The
Healthy Way

As a close friend

of the author, I congratulate Vicky on the publication of this amazing cookbook. Gluten-free diets have become a well-known phenomenon. Gluten sensitivities can be masked by many diseases, preventing people from realizing the cause of their issues. Some resulting neurological disorders include autism, ataxia, severe headaches, ADHD, and OCD. The quality of life for many people has improved as a result of instituting a gluten- and dairy-free and low glycemic diet.

Vicky has been involved for many years in helping families who have members with gluten sensitivity. Her eagerness to give, help others, encourage, and support those with gluten sensitivity has made a tremendous difference. She puts her heart and soul into guiding others, the outcome of which is a dramatic success.

As the Director of Yaldeinu School, a program for children diagnosed with different neurological disorders, especially autism, I implement a complete healthy and gluten- and dairy-free menu. Nutrition is fully incorporated into our program. We also strongly encourage and support our parent body to do the same at home. It has been remarkable to see the resulting beneficial change in our students' behavior and overall health. Eating well, with the proper nutritional foundation, significantly affects both children and adults alike.

I fully commend Vicky for taking on this important responsibility. May the publishing of this book create an awareness of the many wonderful foods one can eat, even when on a gluten-free diet. With the advent of this cookbook, cooking can continue to be a productive and creative activity while remaining within the realm of health and well-being for all.

Mrs. Bluma Bar-Horin, ms

DIRECTOR OF *Yaldeinu School*

Applying The Healthy Way

As my mother~

always taught me, "There are no coincidences," and, accordingly, Vicky showed up in my life exactly when I was ready for her. In 2006, I was faced with the daunting task of figuring out how to provide a gluten-free diet for my sixteen-year-old daughter, who was less than thrilled by this prospect. Vicky was able to guide me through the world of nutritional therapy, and she changed my daughter's life.

The very thought of elimination diets and supplements was overwhelming, but Vicky guided me though slowly and carefully, making sure I was never lost along the way. The attention that I received so lovingly is embodied in the following pages.

With this cookbook, it is no longer difficult to navigate the waters of eating in a healthy, delicious, allergy-free way. This is an invaluable resource for anyone who suffers from food allergies or sensitivities.

I cannot begin to say how grateful I am to have Vicky in my life. She is an upbeat, wonderful teacher, and she works tirelessly to educate the world about holistic living.

I have seen the difference that an allergy (or sensitivity) free diet can make, and my life is better for it. It is no coincidence that Vicky and her incredible cookbook have shown up in your life.

Dr. Aimee Levin Weiner, AuD

The Story Behind The Healthy Way

I'd like to share a story

to welcome you to this book and to the "behind-the-scenes" reason that this book came into being.

About eleven years ago, over five years into my wellness practice and while doing research on celiac disease, I came across an article on gluten sensitivity that I thought would be helpful to at least three of my clients. I suspected that these clients had a gluten sensitivity, but the accepted medical tests of the day showed otherwise. I shared the newly obtained information with my clients. They were very thankful and excited, yet understandably overwhelmed by the specter of dietary restrictions.

In response to their pleas for assistance, I reassured them by saying, "With the help of G-d, we'll swim to shore together."

And what an aquatic feat it turned out to be. The sun's rays glistened on the pristine shores as we dove in, only to be met with threatening waves that came in the form of medical inconsistency and lack of available kosher products. Tides of understanding and then resistance undulated through our journey, but we finally reached shore. The client who had suffered

from Crohn's disease now had a colonoscopy that was clear. The second client's arthritic pain, hormonal imbalance, and chronic fatigue were now controlled. And the third client, who had sudden, unexplained episodes of swelling, difficulty breathing (so much so that she required an EpiPen), and was constantly distracted, could now focus on her exams, and more importantly was EpiPen and medication free.

These three cases are what originally encouraged me to dive into the waters of what was then a vast, virtually unknown area of nutrition. I read constantly and talked to doctors, health practitioners, nutritionists, pediatric therapists, and pedagogical specialists, all to educate myself and arrive here today, just over a decade later.

People choose to live gluten free for a variety of reasons. Whether you have been diagnosed with celiac disease, have a gluten sensitivity, or simply feel better eating gluten-free, the decision to alter your diet is a major transition.

Much has been written about living gluten-free, both from an anecdotal perspective and from a medical perspective. When I started my consultancy practice, eating gluten free was still in its infancy. Now it has grown up, perhaps into adolescence, and we are the main benefactors. My clients have often heard me say, if not once, then many times, "G-d grants me the merit to gather the right information and grants you the merit to make the right decision."

In sum, it's a journey that my clients and I take together. Education is key and must come first. After all the salient information has been put on the table, so to speak, together we translate the "why" into the "how." The "how" is what this book is all about.

And this is what I hope, with all my heart, that this book will provide to you, the reader. The how to feel better.

The recipes in this book are gluten free, dairy free, low glycemic, corn free, and kosher. Wheat, rye, spelt, and barley flour all contain gluten, which is the generic name for certain types of protein contained in these grains. Oats, until recently, was controversial. It is now accepted as an allowed gluten-free grain, if indicated so, meaning that the oats were not grown on the same plantation as other grains. None of my recipes contain wheat flour or flour derived from rye, spelt, or barley.

This book also does not contain any dairy. It's been my experience that many (but certain-ly not all) of those individuals who have gluten sensitivities also possess an intolerance for dairy products (at least while regaining their overall health). Thus, I opted to exclude dairy from this book as well.

It was additionally my intention that the recipes fall low on the glycemic index, which is to say that the dish in question does not rapidly raise your blood sugar. When you peruse the recipes, you will notice many protein choices and many low-glycemic vegetables such as zucchini, broccoli, and the like. Even the two chapters on desserts keep this caveat in mind.

That was quite a challenge. The first order of business was to steer clear of refined sugars and use agave or xylitol in their stead. Only those recipes that could be created with multiple sweeteners grace these pages. I also wanted to make sure that granulated sugar could be used successfully in the same recipe, should my readers prefer it.

The fruit desserts can be made and enjoyed with or without the added sweetener, whichever type you choose to stock. The baking recipes, although they do indeed contain a sweetener of some sort, are much less sweet than their conventional counterparts.

I'd like to take a minute to talk about corn. While corn may not be one of the top eight allergens (peanuts, tree nuts, wheat, milk, eggs, fish, shellfish, and soy), corn allergies are not as uncommon as was once thought.

I had suspected that some of my clients were allergic to corn. Through an elimination diet or testing, those suspicions were confirmed. Symptoms can vary from itchy, watery eyes, hives, and headaches to irritability, indigestion, and poor sleep or fatigue. I made my recipes corn free to service a population and a category that is so little understood and often overlooked. In fact, as of this writing, corn does not fall under the American Consumer Protection Act of 2004, which means that manufacturers are not required to list corn as an ingredient by its common name, highlight it on product labels, or name it as a possible source of cross-contamination.

Although all of the ingredients I call for in this book are corn free, it's important that you check your own products or contact their manufacturers. The items in this book that you need to be careful about are tofu-based products, baking powder, confectioners' sugar, xanthan gum, xylitol, and distilled vinegars.

Since this book is also a kosher cookbook, all of the ingredients called for are kosher certified. Please make sure they meet your standard.

I've talked a lot about what this book does not contain. What it does contain is recipes that use wholesome and natural ingredients. Yes, you have to buy some packaged goods to eat gluten free, such as oat flour or potato starch. But for the most part, these recipes rely on fresh poultry or meat and plenty of fresh vegetables and fruit, not foods that have ingredients which you can't pronounce, let alone recognize.

The book contains recipes that I have made over and over again for my family and friends. Recipes that have been tested thoroughly and have been enjoyed not only in my home but also in the homes of my clients and my friends. I want to assure you that the photos are real. The ingredients were purchased in my neighborhood, the dishes were prepared in my own kitchen and then photographed on a table in my living room. All of the recipes in this book are replicable in your own kitchen, using equipment that you are sure to have on hand and skills that you already possess or can learn easily.

I feel incredibly privileged that my lifelong love of cooking has enabled me to better understand the needs of my clients and respond to them. It is my sincere hope that, as you pursue your health, these recipes will become your family favorites.

VICKY PEARL

Ingredients Unveiled

This introduction

describes those ingredients that are essential to success in the gluten-free kitchen—a kitchen is really not so different from any other, except for some unique items that require explanation.

I often explain to my newly diagnosed clients that most of what they already eat for breakfast, lunch, and dinner can easily be incorporated into an overall healthy gluten-free diet. A quick skim of the following pages will assure you of this truth. Healthy salads and soups, many main dishes, and of course fruits and vegetables of all kinds do not contain gluten. It's when you want a special treat or something different for breakfast or you want to thicken a sauce, for example, that specific knowledge and specific products come into play.

Alternative Flours

All-purpose flour is called that for a very good reason. It has a multitude of uses, from baking breads to creating cookies and cakes, and the list goes on. To achieve baked goods that are similar in texture to those made with wheat flour, a combination of alternative flours is generally used. Most blends, which you can make yourself or buy commercially, combine at least two flours and one or two starches. For this book, I chose several basic flours so that both those new to a gluten-free diet as well as those more familiar with alternative flours could not only have fun baking but could also easily reproduce delicious goodies with a traditional taste and texture.

ALMOND FLOUR

Almond flour is finely ground blanched whole almonds. Although it is sometimes confused with almond meal, the two are in fact quite different. Almond meal has a coarser grind and can be made from unblanched almonds. Please be sure to use only almond flour for the recipes in this book.

Almond flour has a unique, nutty taste and a velvety texture, due to the essential oils found in the almonds. I have found it to be a wonderfully light flour with an airy texture. It is the perfect flour for so many things, among them my Chocolate Chip Cookies, found on page 228. Due to its high oil content, almond flour should be stored in an airtight container in the refrigerator for up to six months. Freeze for longer storage.

Nutritional benefits:

- *High protein content*
- *Monounsaturated (heart healthy) fat*
- *High calcium content*
- *Low glycemic index*
- *High fiber*

OAT FLOUR

Oat flour is made by grinding oats to a fine, extra-fine, medium, or coarse grind. This healthful grain has a similar texture and taste to that of stone-ground whole wheat flour, although it tends to be more bitter. More recently embraced by the gluten-free world than other alternative flours, oat flour can, with much practice, be used on its own in baked goods. It is often combined with other flours to make the item in question a bit lighter. You can also make your own by simply grinding regular oats in the food processor to a fine powder.

If you are lucky enough to come across roasted oats, buy them immediately! Roasting helps sweeten the oats. You can also roast your own oats by spreading them on a baking sheet and roasting them in a 350° oven for five to eight minutes, stirring the oats often. When making the Fluffy Oat Challah on page 190, try to use the finest possible grind of oat flour available.

Oat flour is also my flour of choice when making a roux. I tried several different flours and always seemed to come back to this one, which gives it the correct flavor and texture.

Nutritional benefits:

- *High in fiber*
- *High levels of the B vitamins, vitamin E, calcium, and minerals*

RICE FLOUR

Brown rice flour is milled from unpolished brown rice, which still contains the bran and germ. Accordingly, it is higher in nutrients than white rice flour, whose grains have had the germ and bran removed.

Rice flours are among the most commonly used flours in gluten-free baking. The flour is mild, a creamy brown color, slightly gritty, and often must be used in combination with starches (more on that later). Much like almond flour, brown rice flour will turn rancid if stored at room temperature, due to the inclusion of the bran and germ. Store in an airtight container in the refrigerator for up to one month. Freeze for longer storage.

Nutritional benefits:

- *High fiber*
- *A good source of vitamins and minerals*

SWEET RICE FLOUR

This flour is derived from short-grain glutinous rice such as sushi or sticky rice. As you can see from my chapter on cake and cookies, I tend to use it quite a bit. It's a mild-flavored flour, and unlike its cousin brown rice flour, which tends to have a grainy texture, sweet rice flour has a more sand-like consistency. Because it contains more starch than regular or brown rice, it's more of a cross between a flour and a starch.

Starches

In addition to flours, a well-stocked gluten-free pantry should have different starches on hand. This book relies mainly on potato and tapioca starch. Starch plays a very important role in cooking and baking, since it helps to hold everything together. Of course, other ingredients, such as xanthan gum, yeast, and a combination of flours, can play this role as well. The mild sweetness that starch provides tends to offset the high fiber taste found in many alternative flours.

POTATO STARCH

Potato starch is extracted from potatoes. It is a fine, dry starch with a mild, sweet flavor. In cooking and baking, it adds moistness to baked goods and has a thickening power commensurate to cornstarch. However, it tends to thicken at a lower temperature than cornstarch and results in a glossier and more translucent sauce. It also tends to have a less robust flavor than starches made with corn. Sauces made with potato starch also tend to have a silkier mouthfeel.

Some people shy away from using potato starch due to a belief that it can clump. To this I say, clump you not! Simply dissolve your potato starch in seltzer, and lumps will be a thing of the past.

Potato starch also works wonderfully well as a coating. When a recipe requires a flour coating, as would conventional variations of my Chicken à la Chasseur (see page 110) and Eggplant and Sole Envelopes (see page 132), I simply substitute potato starch for the flour and end up with magnificent results.

TAPIOCA FLOUR

Although billed as a flour, tapioca is in fact considered a starch. It is extracted from the cassava plant. Lower in carbohydrates than potato (which is already low in carbs), it has a mild aftertaste and therefore is best used in combination with flours that have a robust flavor. A quick perusal of the dessert chapters will show you that there are several recipes (among them Rugelach, page 236, and Hamentashen, page 238) where I used both potato and tapioca starch. I did this to help dispel the slight aftertaste of the tapioca. In those recipes where other flavors predominate, such as in the Apple-Blueberry Oat Muffins (see page 224), I only used tapioca.

XANTHAN GUM

You might not believe it, but xanthan gum is a natural carbohydrate. It's made from a microscopic organism called Xanthomonas campestris. After the organism is produced by the fermentation of glucose or sucrose, it is dried and ground into a fine powder and then combined with a liquid to form the gum. Xanthan gum is added to gluten-free baking to mimic the characteristics that protein or gluten naturally provide—that is, viscosity, elasticity, and airiness.

Xanthan gum is very expensive, but you only need to add a little bit of it to derive all of its benefits. If you add too much, your baked goods will be overly elastic and dense. So keep an accurate set of measuring spoons handy. And make sure to mix the xanthan gum thoroughly with your dry ingredients. This way you'll avoid the possible pitfall of ending up with undissolved globs in your cakes and cookies. Store in a cool, dry place for up to one year.

Sweeteners

The gluten-free shelves in the grocery store are fair to bursting with alternative flours and sweeteners. As with the flours that are called for throughout this book, the variety of sweeteners here is condensed to four basic types, although of course there are many possibilities available. Collectively, the recipes require agave, regular granulated sugar, xylitol, and, in a very few cases, honey.

As is mentioned in the introduction, all of the recipes selected for this book have been substantially reduced in terms of their sweetness. I chose agave when I wanted a recipe to fall lower on the glycemic index. Xylitol was offered as a choice for those who have a preference for sugar alcohol or when agave will overly darken a baked good. Sometimes both are offered. In almost every case, refined sugar can be used as a substitute with great success.

AGAVE NECTAR

The nectar of the agave plant, agave is now widely available and can be found in the baking aisle of most supermarkets. Lately, it has become the darling of the baking world, for a few different reasons. Agave falls low on the glycemic index, which means that it is absorbed in the blood stream slowly, thereby preventing spikes in a person's blood sugar. It is also 25 percent sweeter than sugar, which means that you can use less of it to get the same sweet hit. It is also neutrally sweet, making it an ideal choice whether you're cooking with fruit, baking with chocolate, or whisking together a citrus-flavored cake.

Available in a light golden hue or a darker, amber-colored liquid, agave tends to add a lot of moistness to baked goods. With the exception of the Yerushalmi Kugel on page 158, only the light-colored agave was used in this book.

GRANULATED SUGAR

The most common sweetener of all, granulated sugar is highly processed and refined cane or beet sugar. It performs many different functions in baking and cooking. It tenderizes, aerates, colors, and, of course, lends an indefinable sweetness to all manner of baked goods. It is actually considered a liquid ingredient, as sugar dissolves when it comes into contact with water, milk, cream, eggs, and the like.

For those new to a gluten-free diet, it can be an abrupt change to immediately switch to a sweetener like agave when already experimenting with many novel ingredients. In cases like this, I often counsel caution.

Start with switching your all-purpose flour with your chosen alternative flours, but keep using granulated sugar. Then, once you are more accustomed to the texture and taste of gluten-free products, you may choose to introduce agave as your sweetener.

HONEY

Easily digested by the most sensitive of stomachs, honey contains trace amounts of vitamins, minerals, and amino acids. Honey is a bit sweeter than refined sugar, so cup for cup you should be using less. If a recipe calls for 1 cup of granulated sugar, you should use about ¾ cup of honey. However, you may need to alter the amount of liquids in your recipe, so some tampering may be necessary.

XYLITOL

According to the FDA, foods containing sugar alcohols (xylitol, maltitol, and sorbitol) but not sugar can be labeled sugar free, even though they are not calorie free. Generally, these sugar alcohols contain 40 percent fewer calories than sugar. Low on the glycemic index, sugar alcohols tend to have an inconsequential effect on blood glucose and insulin levels.

In this book, xylitol is often called for when I wanted a baked good to retain its light color, as in the Roll Cake (see page 244). Please remember that sugar alcohols should always be used in moderation, since excessive consumption can cause abdominal discomfort or have a laxative effect.

Oils and Other Fats

CANOLA OIL

Throughout this book, I have often called for oil without specifying what kind, with the exception of olive oil (see below). In all of these

cases, when I was developing the recipe or making it for my family, I used canola oil. Because of its neutral taste, canola oil is like a blank canvas, making it the ideal cooking and baking partner. Canola oil is naturally high in monounsaturated fats and low in saturated fat. It's high in omega-3 and a good source of vitamin E.

EXTRA VIRGIN OLIVE OIL

There are recipes scattered throughout this book where I specify to use extra-virgin olive oil. This oil, whether it comes from California, Greece, Spain, Israel, or Italy, enjoys a palette of protective qualities. It is a monounsaturated fat and contains a range of antioxidants, including vitamin E. It's also rich in polyphenols. Consumption of olive oil has also been shown to help improve blood cholesterol levels. It's important to use cold-pressed extra-virgin olive oil, which means that the oil is from the first pressing of the olives, giving it the most flavor, and that no heat has come in touch with the olives.

Extra-virgin olive oil can come in a variety of colors, depending on where the olives were harvested. Generally speaking, the deeper the color of the oil, the more intense the olive flavor. Some are peppery, some are extremely fruity, some are more olive-y. Try different ones and choose the one you like best. Avoid buying "light" olive oil, which tends to come from the last pressing of the olives. It has been more mechanically processed and has the least amount of flavor, although it has the same number of calories.

Olive oil, due to its strong flavor and low smoking point, is best used in salads, baked goods, and marinades, where it doesn't need to be heated to a high heat. It should be stored in a cool, dark, dry place for up to six months. Storage on top of a stove or in direct contact with light can cause the oil to turn rancid. You can refrigerate it if you like. Refrigeration will not change the nutritive value, but the oil will solidify and be unusable without bringing it to room temperature first.

TRANS-FAT-FREE MARGARINE

Trans fats are formed when a liquid vegetable oil undergoes partial hydrogenation, which transforms the oil into a solid fat, such as margarine. Trans fats lower the HDL cholesterol in our bodies, while simultaneously increasing the LDL cholesterol.

There were some recipes that I wanted to include in this book that originally called for regular margarine. After some experimenting, I found that trans-fat-free margarine, made by replacing the otherwise high amounts of hydrogenated oil with other ingredients such as mono- and diglycerides and lecithin, among others, worked really well. The Oatmeal Chocolate Chip Cookies on page 230 simply wouldn't be the same with oil and taste incredibly like the ones I made with regular margarine. The Rugelach on page 236 too came out superbly, easy to roll, flaky, and sweet.

VEGAN BUTTER

Usually a blend of three or more vegetable oils and brought together by a similar process to that of trans-fat-free margarine, vegan

butter works and tastes akin to real butter, but without any dairy components. It is a great substitute for those eliminating dairy butter from their diets who still feel like toast in the morning or a cookie or two in the afternoon.

EGGS

Wherever eggs are called for in the recipes, I used large eggs. I also prefer to use eggs from vegetable-fed, hormone-free, and cage-free hens.

For the purposes of baking, it's important to use only large eggs, as the excess liquid in extra-large eggs will throw off the necessary proportions required, which, after you've spent money on eggs, alternative flours, and sweeteners, can be a heartbreak. In addition, I found that the eggs I used provided a unique bounce that really helped the texture of my gluten-free baked goods.

Some Basic Kitchen Equipment

The following equipment has been used in the recipes in these pages:

A *blender*—the best way to achieve the creamiest soups and the smoothest juice drinks.

A *food processor*—an indispensable kitchen assistant. It simplifies the organization of so many dishes, substantially cutting their preparation time.

An *immersion blender*—a simple yet inexpensive appliance that has so much value. It can puree soups, blend mousses, and aerate other dishes.

Knives—the most useful tools in the kitchen. A variety is handy to have on hand. An 8- or 9-inch chef's knife makes short shrift of chopping and dicing, but be careful, since they can be very sharp. A long serrated knife is best for easily cutting through breads and cakes, while a long thin knife is terrific for slicing meats. Have several small paring knives on hand in your knife block or kitchen drawer.

Measuring cups and spoons—for measuring things like flour or other dry ingredients, you will need a set of stacking dry measures that come in 1-cup, ½-cup, ⅓-cup and ¼-cup measures.

For liquid ingredients, use measuring cups made of tempered glass that have a small spout at the top. They look like small pitchers with measurements of fluid ounces printed on their sides. You will also need one set of graduated measuring spoons.

Parchment paper—a baker's best friend;

eliminates the need to grease pans and helps cookies, biscuits, and crackers slip right off baking sheets. Makes for a much cleaner kitchen.

Spatula—this is extremely valuable for transferring batters from bowls to pans.

Standup mixer—this great appliance can mix ingredients for you, leaving your hands free to do something else.

Wire rack—crucial for allowing baked goods to cool.

Wooden spoons and whisks—it's helpful to have more than one of these handy while baking and cooking.

Some Other Things You Should Know...

Unless otherwise specified, all ingredients are medium sized. This is true for pots and skillets as well.

All the recipes were tested using imperial measurements and a conventional home oven using Fahrenheit settings.

One Last Big Thing

Wanting to change and better one's health is a huge step. And I mean *huge*! It's exciting, daunting, sometimes slightly stressful, and perhaps a little frightening.

What I want more than anything is for people to embrace the change and then not give it up in a couple of weeks out of sheer exasperation. If you give up, not only will you not feel well, but you will feel like a failure too!

This is why I always encourage people to adopt new healthful habits in increments, to see this as a long-term, committed relationship, one that will be successful, with the help of G-d.

I tell people, "I know you wanted to feel better yesterday. In order for that to really happen, we've got to do it slowly."

Invest in new ingredients gradually, two or three at a time, depending on what your pocketbook or budget can afford. Get to know them, their peccadilloes, and how they appeal to you. Then add a few new ones after that. Always

make sure you have enough to eat, both in the refrigerator and in your pantry.

Start with what's familiar to you. This is really important. If you've never eaten fish before, there's no point in starting with fish recipes. If you have made a commitment to try gluten-free pasta and have always loved spaghetti and meatballs, then start with that, not with some exotic combination that you're horrified by but think you should be eating just because it's chockablock full of colorful vegetables. After what may seem like a surprisingly short time, you will be increasingly familiar with novel ingredients—especially those that make you feel better.

If there is just one thing that you take away from this book, it's that this journey is meant to be beautiful and exciting. Beautiful in the sense that it is wonderful to feel as good as you can and to be the most healthful person you can be, and exciting how with the right tools and guidance, your story can be exhilaratingly successful.

Appetizers and dips

are a delicious way to welcome friends and family into your home and to your dinner table. They capture the host's spirit of generosity and the desire to please whomever is invited to share in the repast. The dips included in this chapter are meant to enhance that experience of gathering together and eating side by side. They not only whet the appetite but also provide a sound nutritional base, whether they are the preface to a meal or simply an afternoon nosh. Relying as they do on a cornucopia of good natural foods, bursting with nutrients, they are meant to optimize your health and excite your senses.

And, let's face it, kids respond to this sense of excitement just as keenly as adults do. Make sure that your vegetables explode with color and variety. Take the time to create some funny faces or vivid scenes that will attract children and make them want to munch on a carrot and dip a celery stick into a nutrient-savvy Eggplant Dip. If it's true that we eat with our eyes before we even taste a morsel, then it's all the more reason to let your inner artist out and create a magnificent dip spread.

The fruit-based drinks included in this chapter are fun yet brimming with nutrients. They're light and not too filling, leaving your guests' appetites intact for the main course.

Delicious Dips & Drinks~

Creamy Eggplant Dip

Yield 1½ cups

With a bit of effort, you'll have a rich, creamy spread or dip... Just be sure to make enough!

Ingredients

1	LARGE EGGPLANT
1	SMALL CLOVE GARLIC
2 Tbsp	*(heaping)* MAYONNAISE
1 tsp	AGAVE, XYLITOL, OR GRANULATED SUGAR
½ tsp	KOSHER SALT, *plus more for sprinkling*
¼ tsp	FRESHLY GROUND BLACK PEPPER

Directions

1 Without slicing all the way through, cut a lengthwise slit in the eggplant. Double-wrap well in aluminum foil.

2 Place eggplant directly on stove over medium heat. Cook, turning every few minutes, until sides are very soft. Remove from heat and let cool slightly. Place in a strainer and slowly unwrap foil. With a large spoon, scoop out the inside and discard peel.

3 Sprinkle some salt on eggplant while still in strainer. Let strain for 5 minutes.

4 Place strained eggplant in the bowl of a food processor fitted with the metal "S" blade attachment; add remaining ingredients. Blend until creamy.

Tip: *When purchasing eggplant, choose one that is lightweight. This will ensure that the eggplant is ripe and less bitter.*

Don't *forget to consider texture when preparing a meal or even just putting out an assortment of appetizers. Pair this smooth and creamy dip with crunchy Almond Crackers (see page 198) or perhaps some carrot sticks and juicy celery pieces.*

Falafel Balls

These falafel balls are not only delicious; you would also never know that they are gluten free. To make them into a filling dinner, serve in Wraps (see page 194), accompanied with Hummus (see page 29) and Guacamole.

Ingredients

1 LB	CHICKPEAS *(garbanzo beans)*
1	HEAD GARLIC *(about 12 cloves, peeled)*
1	LARGE ONION
3	LARGE EGGS
1 TBSP	DRIED CILANTRO LEAVES
1 TSP	FRESHLY GROUND BLACK PEPPER
1 TBSP	KOSHER SALT
1 TBSP	BAKING SODA
1 TBSP	GROUND CUMIN
2 CUPS	WATER
1 CUP	GLUTEN-FREE OAT MATZAH MEAL *(plus more if needed)*
•	OIL, *for frying*

Directions

1 Soak chickpeas in water overnight, or for a quick alternative, place in a large pot filled with 3 inches of water. Bring to a boil and boil for 3 minutes. Remove from heat and let stand, covered, for 1 hour. Drain.

2 In the bowl of a food processor fitted with the metal "S" blade attachment, grind the beans, garlic cloves, and onion. Place mixture in a large bowl and combine with remaining ingredients.

3 Cover bowl with plastic wrap and refrigerate for at least 1 hour or until firm enough to form small balls. Fill a saucepan more than halfway with oil. Heat over high heat.

4 Wet your hands. Form chickpea mixture into walnut-sized balls, adding additional matzah meal if mixture is too loose to hold together.

5 Cook balls in hot oil, turning occasionally, for 5 to 10 minutes, or until balls turn a golden brown. Remove with slotted spoon and drain on paper towel.

Matzah *meal was the best choice of flour for these balls. All the other flours I tried—and I tried several—didn't give me the same results, especially once they were frozen. Brown rice flour worked well when the falafel balls were made fresh, but turned heavy and dry once refrigerated or frozen. Oat flour, for which I had high hopes, resulted in the same too-dense texture when made ahead.*

Tip:
*To prevent
the balls from
sticking to the
bottom of the
pot during fry-
ing, place a few
slices of raw
carrot or a few
baby carrots in
the pot.*

*This mixture
freezes well for
up to 6 months.
You can divide
into smaller
containers so
you don't have
to make 50
balls at once.
Be sure to add
a bit of matzah
meal when
mixture has
thawed.*

Tehina typically partners with falafel balls; however, it's great as a salad dressing or as a dip for vegetable sticks.

Tehina

Ingredients

1 CUP	TAHINI *(sesame paste)*
1 CUP	WATER
3 TBSP	FRESHLY SQUEEZED LEMON JUICE
1 TSP	KOSHER SALT
2 TBSP	AGAVE OR GRANULATED SUGAR
2	CLOVES GARLIC

Directions

- In the bowl of a food processor fitted with the metal "S" blade attachment, blend all ingredients together on high speed for 2 minutes.

Tip: *You may add more water for a more liquid consistency.*

Tahini *is highly perishable, so be sure to keep your jar refrigerated. As it sits in the refrigerator, the natural oils (which are happily the ones that are good for you) will rise to the top of the jar. Just give a quick stir to mix it back together. The acid in the lemon juice thickens the sesame seed paste, so if you make your tahina ahead, you may need to thin it out with some more lemon juice or water.*

Hummus

You may never purchase a store-bought hummus again once you experience an authentic homemade version.

Directions

1 Place all ingredients in the bowl of a food processor with a metal "S" blade attachment.

2 Blend until almost smooth.

Ingredients

1½ CUPS	COOKED CHICKPEAS *(cooked garbanzo beans)* OR 1 CAN *(15½ oz)* CHICKPEAS, drained well and rinsed
¼ CUP	WATER *(½ cup if you like a runny consistency)*
2½ TBSP	FRESHLY SQUEEZED LEMON JUICE
2 TBSP	TAHINI *(sesame paste)*
2 TBSP	EXTRA-VIRGIN OLIVE OIL
1	SMALL GARLIC CLOVE
1 TBSP	DRIED PARSLEY LEAVES
1 TSP	KOSHER SALT
¼ TSP	GROUND CUMIN

Tip: *For that special touch, top with 2 tsp extra-virgin olive oil, pine nuts, and a sprinkle of paprika.*

Packed *with protein and an excellent source of fiber, hummus is an ideal choice for a snack along with vegetable sticks, over a salad, or perhaps along with some Crispy Crackers (see page 196).*

Simple & Elegant Dips

Yield Olive Dip: ½ cup
Pickle Dip: ½ cup
Tomato Dip: ¾ cup

What better way to greet your guests than with these simple, straightforward dips that are both delicious and easy to make ahead?

Ingredients

Olive Dip

¼ CUP	PITTED OLIVES
½ CUP	MAYONNAISE
2	CLOVES GARLIC, *crushed*

Pickle Dip

2	LARGE SOUR PICKLES
½ CUP	MAYONNAISE
2	CLOVES GARLIC
¼ CUP	PICKLE JUICE

Tomato Dip

3	VINE-RIPENED TOMATOES
1	CLOVE GARLIC
½ TSP	KOSHER SALT
⅛ TSP	FRESHLY GROUND BLACK PEPPER, *optional*
¼ CUP	OIL

Directions

Olive and Pickle Dips

- In a blender, blend all ingredients together on high speed for 3 minutes or until it reaches the desired consistency.

Tomato Dip

1. Place tomatoes, garlic, and spices in a blender. Blend ingredients together on high speed.

2. Add oil and continue blending for 3 minutes or until it reaches the desired consistency.

3. Shake well before serving.

The *pickle dip recipe can be made with full fat or light mayonnaise, and no one will be the wiser. Homemade mayonnaise is a breeze to make, especially when you make it in a food processor, like I do. Try my homemade version, found on page 33.*

For *tomato dips, salsas, or bruschetta toppings, make sure to choose beefsteak tomatoes, which are juicier than Roma tomatoes. Fresh tomatoes should be firm, but give slightly to gentle pressure. They should feel heavy for their size and not have any signs of mold or bruising.*

Try *stirring some finely grated lemon zest into the olive dip for a citrusy flavor. Or, if you like spice, sprinkle a hint of dried red pepper flakes on top. The earthy flavor of finely chopped fresh rosemary marries especially well with the olives.*

Garlic Dip

Works well with salmon, crackers, challah, and more.

Ingredients

½ CUP	MAYONNAISE
2	CLOVES GARLIC, *crushed*
½ TSP	KOSHER SALT
⅛ TSP	MUSTARD SPICE, *optional*

Directions

- Mix all ingredients together with a fork.

Avoid *storing fresh garlic in the refrigerator. It's best to store in a terra-cotta container with holes on top that allows the garlic to breathe, preferably in a cool, dry place. Kept away from moisture and humidity, garlic will keep for up to 8 weeks as a whole head, and once broken into cloves will keep for 3 to 10 days. Should you find yourself out of fresh garlic, this dip can be successfully mixed together with 2 tsp of garlic powder instead.*

Homemade Mayonnaise

Yield *2 cups*

This is the recipe I use for all the recipes in this cookbook that include mayonnaise. I prefer to keep it simple, without adding lemon juice, vinegar, or sugar.

When *you make mayonnaise at home, you get to be in the driver's seat. You can choose the heart-healthy neutral-flavored oil (I use canola) without the addition of preservatives.*

Directions

1 Place eggs and salt in the bowl of a food processor fitted with the metal "S" blade attachment.

2 With machine running on high speed, gradually pour in oil. Continue beating on the highest speed for 3 to 4 minutes, or until it reaches the consistency of store-bought mayonnaise.

3 Mayonnaise can be stored in an airtight container in the refrigerator for up to 2 weeks.

Ingredients

2	LARGE EGGS
1 TSP	KOSHER SALT
2 CUPS	OIL

Blueberry Spritz

An impressive, refreshing champagne.

Ingredients

5 CUPS	SELTZER
¼ CUP	SEMIDRY RED WINE
1 TSP	BLACK CHERRY SYRUP *(health food store brand), optional*
1 CUP	FRESH BLUEBERRIES
1 CUP	WATER

Directions

1. Pour seltzer, wine, and syrup, if using, into a pitcher. Mix gently and refrigerate until ice cubes are ready.

2. Divide blueberries among the compartments of an ice-cube tray.

3. Pour enough water into each compartment to just cover the blueberries.

4. Freeze for 4 hours or until firm.

5. Once firm, add ice cubes to pitcher.

When *developing recipes for this book, I knew I wanted to include a few drinks. I also wanted those drinks to have some fruit in them for a healthy slant, and to be pretty enough to pass muster for special occasions. First I developed the idea of freezing blueberries in ice-cube trays. Then came the idea of the red wine mixed with seltzer, and then came the idea of cherry syrup to heighten the red wine color. Put it altogether, and you have a sparkling winner of a drink.*

Mango & Pomegranate Drink

Yield *4 cups*

This "pick-me-up" drink offers a wonderful burst of nutrients, color, and flavor.

Ingredients

2   MANGOES, *peeled, pitted, and diced*

2   ORANGES, *freshly squeezed*

1 CUP   POMEGRANATE ARILS *(from 1 large pomegranate)*

1 CUP   WATER

Directions

1   Place diced mangoes in a blender and blend until it reaches a smooth consistency.

2   Add orange juice and blend well. Refrigerate.

3   Divide pomegranate seeds evenly among the compartments of an ice-cube tray. Pour in enough water to just cover the seeds. Freeze for 4 hours or until firm.

4   Once firm, add ice cubes to pitcher.

Mangoes *contain a special enzyme that can be a soothing digestive aid. If only underripe mangoes are available, place them in a paper bag and store in a cool, dark place for a few days until they ripen.*

Refreshing Summer Drink

Yield **6 cups**

This thick, orange-hued smoothie freckled with small pieces of strawberry is as refreshing in the morning as it is in the afternoon.

Ingredients

- 2   LARGE RIPE MANGOES, *peeled, pitted, and diced*

- 8   LARGE RIPE PEACHES, *peeled, pitted, and sliced into wedges*

- 2 BOXES   FRESH STRAWBERRIES, *stems removed and halved (or 1 16-oz package frozen)*

Directions

- Place fruit in a blender or the bowl of a food processor fitted with the metal "S" blade attachment and blend until it reaches a smooth consistency.

I chose mango for this smoothie due to its rich antioxidants. Peaches and strawberries are a great source of vitamin C as well. But you can also use whatever ripe fruit you have in your fridge or on your countertop. The deeper the color, the higher the nutrients.

You might not have

thought of it this way, but to me there is a salad pendulum. Salads were once a simple affair, a plate of greens with a simple dressing, placed at the side of your plate or perhaps even served toward the end of a meal. All in all, an uninspiring approach to eating your daily quotient of greens. Then the pendulum swung sharply to the other end, where salads became the recipient of every vegetable and legume imaginable, with an assortment of flowers and proteins stacked on top.

For me, salads are a great part of the meal and can even be a simple meal on their own. I look to the vegetables themselves for leadership and always come away inspired. You'll find that my salads tend to focus on one or two vegetables and use a simple dressing that optimizes the natural integrity of those particular goodies. Some are side salads, such as the **Hearts of Palm** or the **Cucumber Salad**. But there's plenty of room for improvisation. If you want to make a complete meal out of these salads, feel free to add some chickpeas or sliced cooked chicken. This is particularly true of the pasta salads, which are filling and can easily do double duty as a lunch or dinner. So pick a comfortable spot on the pendulum and enjoy!

Sensational Salads

Lettuce– Avocado Salad

This simple salad is ideal when you're short on time and you don't want your family's dinner to fall short in taste or nutritional value.

Ingredients

4 CUPS	CHOPPED, WASHED ROMAINE LETTUCE *(1 8-oz bag)*
2 CUPS	CHERRY TOMATOES, *halved (1 pint)*
2	RIPE AVOCADOS, *peeled and diced*

Dressing

2 TBSP	EXTRA-VIRGIN OLIVE OIL
½–¾ TSP	KOSHER SALT
2	CLOVES GARLIC, *minced*

Directions

- Place vegetables in a serving bowl. In a separate small bowl, mix together dressing ingredients. Pour over vegetables, tossing gently until well coated.

Once *you cut into an avocado, its flesh will start to discolor quickly. To prevent discoloration, brush sliced avocado or toss chopped avocado with an acid such as vinegar, lemon juice, or lime juice. Coating with oil will also act as a barrier. Be sure to choose heavy avocados with unblemished skin. Avocados that are ready to use will yield slightly to gentle pressure. Avoid those that have soft spots, which may indicate bruising or overripeness. If you can only find hard avocados, place inside a paper bag with a banana and your avocados will be ready for use within a day or two.*

Tip: *The best way to cut an avocado is to cut in half lengthwise to the pit. Then twist to separate the two halves. Hit the pit with the knife until it is slightly embedded. Twist the knife to remove pit.*

If *your family is still new to healthy eating and to the taste of extra-virgin olive oil, begin with ½ Tbsp olive oil and 1½ Tbsp of a neutral-tasting oil.*

Avocados *are a rich source of heart-healthy monounsaturated fats. The creamier the inside of the avocado, the higher the fat content.*

Beet Salad

Frozen cooked beets have all sorts of wonderful benefits, and they're great as a backup side dish, which can be as simple as serving them with a squeeze of fresh lemon or lime juice. This salad lets them sing in all their natural exuberance.

Ingredients

10	BEETS, *peeled*
1	RED ONION, *finely sliced*

Dressing

½ CUP	LIQUID FROM COOKED BEETS OR WATER
⅓ CUP	VINEGAR OR FRESHLY SQUEEZED LEMON JUICE
¼ CUP	AGAVE, XYLITOL, OR GRANULATED SUGAR
¼ CUP	OIL
2 TSP	KOSHER SALT
½ TSP	FRESHLY GROUND BLACK PEPPER

Directions

1 Place beets in an 8–10-quart pot (depending on size of beets); cover with water. Bring to a rolling boil over high heat. Cook for 1 to 2 hours, maintaining a rolling boil, or until beets are tender enough that the tines of a fork meet with little resistance. Reserving ½ cup of cooking water, remove beets from water. Cool slightly. Slice beets according to your preference.

2 Place beets in a serving bowl; add onions. In a separate small bowl, mix together dressing ingredients. Pour dressing over vegetables, tossing gently until well coated. For best results, cover with plastic wrap and refrigerate overnight. Bring to room temperature before serving.

Tip: *Try to buy beets that are uniform in size, since they'll cook more evenly that way. As an added bonus, smaller beets are sweeter.*

Beets *come in a variety of different colors such as golden or white, in addition to the classic deep red. The latter is the highest in nutrients. Betaine, the natural compound that gives beets their characteristic hue, is a more potent antioxidant than polyphenol in lowering blood pressure. It is also an excellent source of fiber, and its high levels of nitrates work like aspirin to prevent blood clots.*

Broccoli & Carrot Salad

A refreshing change from your usual lettuce salad. A vegetable combo at its best!

Ingredients

1½ LB   FROZEN BROCCOLI FLORETS, *thawed*

3   CARROTS, *grated*

Dressing

¼–½ CUP   MAYONNAISE *(you be the judge)*

½ TSP   KOSHER SALT

¼ TSP   GARLIC POWDER

⅛ TSP   ONION POWDER

Directions

- In a serving bowl, combine broccoli and carrots. In a separate small bowl, stir together dressing ingredients. Pour dressing over vegetables, tossing gently until well coated.

As *with most vegetables, the darker the color, the higher the nutrients. Broccoli, a prominent member of the cruciferous family, is high in flavonoids and is an excellent source of vitamin C, calcium, folate, and fiber. A nutritional all-star, to say the least.*

Cabbage & Angel-Hair Pasta Salad

Yield *8 to 10 servings*

A salad that has made a gluten-free dish a hero once again! The purple cabbage not only provides a lovely color but is also satisfying and filling, while the toasted almonds provide just the right amount of crunch.

Ingredients

1 BAG	*(16 oz)* BROWN RICE ANGEL-HAIR PASTA *(or spaghetti)*
1 CUP	SLIVERED ALMONDS
4 CUPS	SHREDDED PURPLE CABBAGE *(about 1 lb)*
4–5	SCALLIONS, *thinly sliced*

Dressing

½ CUP	AGAVE, XYLITOL, OR GRANULATED SUGAR
⅓ CUP	VINEGAR
⅓ CUP	OIL
2 TSP	KOSHER SALT
½ TSP	FRESHLY GROUND BLACK PEPPER

Directions

1 Bring a large pot of water set over high heat to just under a boil, just to the point where small bubbles form. Sprinkle in some salt. Break pasta into pot. Cook uncovered, stirring occasionally, for 12 minutes. Drain pasta well; rinse under cold water to stop the cooking process. Place pasta in a large bowl.

2 In a small bowl, stir together dressing ingredients. Pour dressing over pasta, and let marinate at room temperature for at least 1 hour or up to 3 hours.

3 Meanwhile, scatter slivered almonds on a parchment-paper-lined cookie sheet. Toast in a preheated 350° oven, stirring them halfway through cooking time, for 10 to 15 minutes or until golden and crisp.

4 Just before serving, stir cabbage and scallions into pasta. Sprinkle with almonds.

Tip: *If you have leftover cabbage, either the preshredded variety or part of a whole cabbage, wrap well, refrigerate, and use within three to four days.*

To *preserve the vitamin C content of your cabbage, store it in the coldest part of your refrigerator. Vitamin C will start to break down if the cabbage is stored in a warm environment. Red cabbage, the main component of the salad above, has higher levels of vitamin C, beta-carotene, calcium, and minerals than lighter-colored cabbage.*

Caesar Salad

Yield *4 to 6 servings*

Quick to prepare and quick to disappear.

Ingredients

4 CUPS	CHOPPED, WASHED ROMAINE LETTUCE *(1 8-oz bag)*
2 CUPS	GRAPE TOMATOES, *sliced lengthwise*
1½ CUPS	SLICED PICKLES *(either brined or sour)*
4	SCALLIONS, *sliced, optional*

Dressing

4 Tbsp	MAYONNAISE
¼ CUP	PICKLE JUICE
1 TSP	GARLIC POWDER
½ TSP	KOSHER SALT
⅛ TSP	MUSTARD POWDER, *optional*

Directions

1. In a large serving bowl, toss vegetables together.

2. In a separate small bowl, stir together dressing ingredients.

3. Pour dressing over vegetables, tossing gently until well coated. Serve immediately.

Romaine *lettuce, the crunchy lettuce synonymous with Caesar salad, is just one of the dozens of varieties of leafy greens available now. Romaine provides five times as much vitamin C and is higher in beta-carotene than iceberg lettuce. It's also low in calories and is a wonderful canvas for a multitude of flavorful dressings. As an added bonus, it's high in fiber.*

Potato Salad

"I just can't make enough of it" is the comment I get time and time again after sharing this recipe. The pickle juice in the dressing makes a world of difference. Try it, you'll see what I mean.

Ingredients

10	LARGE RED POTATOES
5	LARGE SOUR PICKLES, *diced (or 2 cups diced)*
1	SMALL RED ONION, *diced*
1	SMALL CARROT, *finely grated or diced*

Dressing

6 TBSP	*(heaping)*	MAYONNAISE
⅓ CUP	SOUR PICKLE JUICE	
1 TSP	KOSHER SALT	

Directions

1. Wash potatoes, scrubbing clean. Place in a large pot; fill with water to just cover potatoes. Bring to a boil over high heat. Cook over high heat, maintaining a rolling boil, for 30 minutes or until potatoes are fork tender.

2. Drain potatoes; peel and cool slightly. Cut into cubes and place in a large bowl.

3. Add pickles, red onion, and carrot to bowl. In a separate small bowl, mix together dressing ingredients. Pour dressing over vegetables, tossing gently until well coated.

This *is the ultimate make-once, eat-two-to-three-times mother's-helper salad. It's wonderful the first night just the way it is. The next night, it's terrific as a side dish, with some chopped red and green peppers tossed in. If there's some left over after that, add a chopped hard-boiled egg for a light but nutritious lunch.*

An all-time favorite!

Coleslaw

Ingredients

1 BAG   *(16 oz)* SHREDDED COLESLAW MIX *(4 cups shredded cabbage plus ⅛ cup shredded carrots)*

Dressing

½ CUP   WATER

¼ CUP   XYLITOL OR GRANULATED SUGAR

3 TBSP *(heaping)* MAYONNAISE

1 TBSP VINEGAR

2 TSP   KOSHER SALT

¼ TSP   GARLIC POWDER

⅛ TSP   ONION POWDER

Directions

1 Place coleslaw mix in a large serving bowl.

2 In a separate small bowl, mix together dressing ingredients.

3 Pour dressing over coleslaw mix, tossing until well coated.

4 For best results, cover with plastic wrap and refrigerate overnight. Bring to room temperature before serving.

Take *inspiration from your neighborhood restaurant and turn leftover coleslaw (should there happen to be any) into a special luncheon for one. Mound some coleslaw on your plate. Top with a thinly sliced chicken cutlet or a scoop of tuna or egg salad. Sprinkle with a bit of chopped fresh parsley. Remember, you're making this for yourself and you're pretty special. Sit down, take a deep breath, and enjoy!*

Cucumber Salad

Yield *8 servings*

A light, refreshing accompaniment to fish, chicken, or meat. A classic well received every and any time!

Typically, *store-bought cucumber salads contain loads of sugar. This recipe contains a fragment of that amount. If you want to lower the sugar content even further, simply combine ⅓ cup xylitol or granulated sugar with ⅓ cup freshly squeezed lemon juice in a small pot. Bring mixture to a boil over medium-high heat. Remove from heat immediately. Let cool and toss with cucumbers and onions.*

Directions

1 Peel cucumbers; slice into thin slices. Place in a large bowl. Slice onion into thin slices and place in a separate large bowl.

2 Sprinkle salt over cucumbers; stir gently to distribute salt. Let stand for at least 30 minutes or up to 1 hour. (This will extract the bitterness.)

3 With your hands, squeeze handfuls of cucumbers at a time to extract as much excess liquid as possible. Rinse cucumbers under cold water; drain well. Add cucumbers to the bowl with the onions. Mix in xylitol and vinegar, tossing gently until well coated. For best results, cover with plastic wrap and refrigerate overnight. Bring to room temperature before serving.

Ingredients

10	PERSIAN CUCUMBERS
1 TSP	*(heaping)* KOSHER SALT, *for sprinkling*
1	ONION
⅔ CUP	XYLITOL OR GRANULATED SUGAR
⅓ CUP	VINEGAR OR FRESHLY SQUEEZED LEMON JUICE

Eggplant Salad

A light, flavorful version of a Middle Eastern classic.

Ingredients

¼ CUP	OIL
2	EGGPLANTS, *unpeeled and diced*
2	TOMATOES, *diced*
4	PICKLES IN BRINE *(sour pickles can be substituted), diced*
1	RED PEPPER, *thinly sliced lengthwise or diced*
½ CUP	SLICED GREEN OLIVES *(pitted or stuffed)*
2	CLOVES GARLIC, *crushed*
2 TBSP	VINEGAR
1 TSP	KOSHER SALT

Directions

1 Heat oil in a pan set over medium heat. Add diced eggplant and sauté for about 10 minutes or until soft. Transfer eggplant to paper towel; drain well.

2 Place remaining ingredients in a large bowl; add eggplant. Mix together gently. For best results, cover with plastic wrap and refrigerate overnight. Bring to room temperature before serving.

As *with beets, try to buy smaller-sized eggplants—the smaller ones tend to be less bitter. When checking for ripeness, don't hesitate to apply pressure to an eggplant. If it has a slight give and bounces back, this is the one you want. If the indentation remains, the eggplant is overripe (put that one back in the bin). Alternatively, if there is no give, then the eggplant was picked too early (skip that one). If it sounds hollow, it will be dry inside (skip that one too).*

Full-of-Color Pasta Salad

A bright and tasty salad that is high in fiber to boot!

Ingredients

1 BAG	*(16 oz)* TRI-COLORED BROWN RICE SPIRAL PASTA
1	RED ONION, *diced*
1	RED PEPPER, *diced*
1	YELLOW PEPPER, *diced*
1	CARROT, *diced*
2	STALKS CELERY, *diced*

Dressing

½ CUP	AGAVE, XYLITOL, OR GRANULATED SUGAR
⅓ CUP	VINEGAR
⅓ CUP	OIL
2 TSP	KOSHER SALT
½ TSP	FRESHLY GROUND BLACK PEPPER

Directions

1. Bring a large pot of water set over high heat to just under a boil, just to the point where small bubbles form. Sprinkle in some salt. Add pasta to pot. Cook uncovered, stirring occasionally, for 12 minutes. Drain pasta well; rinse under cold water to stop the cooking process.

2. Place pasta in a large bowl. Add vegetables and mix well.

3. In a small bowl, mix together dressing ingredients. Pour dressing over pasta and vegetables, tossing gently until well coated.

4. For best results, cover with plastic wrap and refrigerate for up to 3 hours. Bring to room temperature before serving.

Wherever *they are arranged on the rainbow, peppers contain high levels of carotene, antioxidants including vitamins C and E, and lutein, and are a great source of B6 and folate. The brighter the color, the richer the source of nutrients.*

Hearts OF Palm Salad

Hearts of palm are so scrumptious that they need little, if any, embellishment. However, paired with slices of tomatoes and topped with just a dash of oil and salt, they become a satisfying costar to the main event.

Ingredients

10	HEARTS OF PALM, *finely sliced (about 2 jars)*
2	BEEFSTEAK TOMATOES OR 6 PLUM TOMATOES, *finely sliced*
2 TBSP	OIL
1 TBSP	DRIED PARSLEY LEAVES
•	KOSHER SALT, *to taste*

Directions

- In a large bowl, mix together hearts of palm, tomatoes, oil, dried parsley, and salt to taste. Enjoy!

This *salad, although sparse in ingredients, packs a punch on the satisfaction scale. And, as we all know, once you're satisfied, you're less likely to be tempted by foods that fall lower on the nutritional value continuum.*

Marinated Vegetable Salad

Crispy, healthy, and satisfying, this salad is a riot of color and crunch.

Ingredients

- 2 YELLOW PEPPERS, *finely sliced*
- 2 RED PEPPERS, *finely sliced*
- 1 GREEN PEPPER, *finely sliced*
- 2 ZUCCHINI (*unpeeled*), *finely sliced*
- 2 CARROTS, *peeled and finely sliced*
- 1 RED ONION, *finely sliced*
- ½ LB FROZEN BROCCOLI FLORETS, *thawed, optional*

Dressing

- ⅓ CUP VINEGAR
- ¼ CUP AGAVE, XYLITOL, OR GRANULATED SUGAR
- ¼ CUP OIL
- ½ TSP KOSHER SALT
- ¼ TSP FRESHLY GROUND BLACK PEPPER

Directions

1 Place all vegetables in a large bowl.

2 In a separate small bowl, mix together dressing ingredients. Pour dressing over vegetables, tossing gently until well coated.

3 For best results, cover with plastic wrap and refrigerate overnight. Bring to room temperature before serving.

Did *you know that all peppers start off green? Then, depending on the seed, they will grow to be red, yellow, orange, purple, or even black. Red peppers are simply green peppers that are ripened for a longer period of time. It's also why they're sweeter. Green peppers are harvested before they are ripe, so they are less sweet and not as expensive.*

Quick & Easy Pasta Salad

Yield *6 servings*

A wholesome, nutritious dish with the added bonus of being kid-friendly.

Ingredients

1 BAG	*(16 oz)* BROWN RICE SPIRAL PASTA
½	SMALL GREEN PEPPER, *diced*
½	SMALL RED PEPPER, *diced*
4	LARGE SOUR PICKLES, *diced (or 1¾ cup)*

Dressing

3 TBSP	*(heaping)* MAYONNAISE
1½ CUPS	SOUR PICKLE JUICE
1 TSP	KOSHER SALT

Directions

1 Bring a large pot of water set over high heat to just under a boil, just to the point where small bubbles form. Sprinkle in some salt. Add pasta to pot. Cook uncovered, stirring occasionally, for 12 minutes. Drain pasta well; rinse under cold water to stop the cooking process.

2 Place pasta in a large serving bowl. Stir in peppers and pickles.

3 In a small bowl, stir together dressing ingredients. Pour dressing over pasta mixture, tossing gently until well coated.

4 For best results, cover with plastic wrap and refrigerate for up to 3 hours. Bring to room temperature before serving.

Become *a pasta expert! Different shapes of pasta are classically paired with certain types of sauces. For example, thin strands of pasta such as angel-hair pasta or spaghetti are paired with silky tomato or cream sauces. Spirals are often combined with a chunkier sauce, so that the happy eater can get a trapped morsel in every bite.*

Soups really are

super for so many reasons. First, they're easy on the cook and very forgiving—one of the easiest things you can concoct in a kitchen. I happen to love them for their versatility. There's nothing quite as comforting as a homemade chicken soup, its golden liquid sending a rich aroma throughout the house, its mellow broth both soothing and invigorating.

Soups can be light and delicately flavored, like my **Cream of Zucchini**, made creamy by the addition of potatoes, or hearty and satisfying, as in the case of the **Vegetable Soup** or the **Split Pea Soup with Dumplings**. Soups can be the way you introduce a new vegetable or hide it if you have picky eaters at home. It's the place you get to be creative too, substituting whatever may be called for in a recipe with vegetables more to your liking or those that need to be used up in your refrigerator. You can't go wrong with soup!

Super
Soups

Chicken Soup & Knaidlach

A golden remedy, a golden tradition, a golden taste…with an innovative twist. For years, I made chicken soup the traditional way: I brought all my ingredients to a boil in a large pot of water and then simmered it all for a couple of hours. Then a friend shared an altogether new method.

Ingredients

Chicken Soup

1	WHOLE CHICKEN, *cut in quarters*
2 LB	CHICKEN OR TURKEY BONES, *placed in a Wrap 'n Boil bag*
4	CARROTS, *peeled and cut into chunks*
5	STALKS CELERY, *cut into chunks*
1	LARGE ONION
1	SMALL ZUCCHINI, *peeled, cut in chunks*
1	SMALL SWEET POTATO, *peeled and cut in chunks, optional*
1	HANDFUL FRESH PARSLEY LEAVES
1	LARGE PARSLEY ROOT, *peeled*
1 Tbsp	*(heaping)* KOSHER SALT

Knaidlach

4	LARGE EGGS
¼ CUP	OIL
½ CUP	WATER OR SELTZER
1½ CUPS	GLUTEN-FREE OAT MATZAH MEAL
½ TSP	KOSHER SALT

Directions

Chicken Soup

1 Fill a 10-quart pot with water. Bring to a boil over high heat. Carefully add all ingredients to pot. Bring quickly back to a boil.

2 Reduce heat to medium-high; cook, with lid slightly ajar, for 2 hours.

Freezes very well for up to six months. Chill before freezing and thaw in refrigerator.

Knaidlach

1 In a bowl, stir together eggs, oil, water, matzah meal, and salt with a fork. Refrigerate, uncovered, for about 2 hours, or freeze until firm.

2 Bring a pot of water (or soup) to a boil. If using water, add a bit of salt.

If you prefer your matzah balls on the light and fluffy side, use seltzer and simmer the matzah balls covered. If, on the other hand, you prefer your matzah balls slightly heavier, use water as your liquid of choice and simmer uncovered.

Tip: *By bringing the water to a boil on its own, and only then adding the rest of the ingredients, you are virtually guaranteed a crystal-clear chicken soup.*

Although *I adore fresh chicken soup, I also enjoy the reassurance of having plenty on hand in my freezer. I try to always use fresh chicken parts for my soup, as fresh imparts a golden color to the broth, whereas frozen chicken parts tend not to. If you prefer to use chicken bones, it doesn't seem to matter if they're fresh or frozen.*

3 With wet hands, form matzah meal mixture into walnut-sized balls. You will have about 15 balls. Drop into boiling water or soup. Reduce heat and simmer, covered, for 15 to 20 minutes or until cooked through.

This recipe has a special place in my heart. It's a gluten-free version of a traditional dish that tastes exactly like my grandmother's.

Kreplach

Ingredients

1 CUP	BROWN RICE FLOUR
1 CUP	TAPIOCA FLOUR
½ CUP	POTATO STARCH
1 TSP	XANTHAN GUM
2	LARGE EGGS
½ CUP	WATER
½ CUP	OIL
•	PINCH OF KOSHER SALT

Filling

5	GRILLED PATTIES, *mashed (see page 98)*

Directions

1 In a mixer fitted with the dough hook, mix together dough ingredients until well combined.

2 Roll dough between two well-floured pieces of parchment paper to ⅛-inch thickness. Cut into 3x3-inch squares.

3 Place 1 heaping tsp of filling onto each square. Fold dough over filling, forming a triangle. Press edges with the tines of a fork to seal.

4 Fill an 8-quart pot to a little bit more than ¾ full with water; bring to a boil over high heat. Add ⅛ tsp salt.

5 One at a time, add kreplach to boiling water. Return to a rolling boil. Reduce heat to medium-low. Cook, covered, for 20 minutes.

6 Without letting kreplach fall out, pour out hot water from pot. Refill with cold water, making sure that the water completely covers all the kreplach. Allow kreplach to cool in water. Remove using a slotted spoon.

7 Add to soup, heat thoroughly, and enjoy.

These freeze very well for up to 6 months. Chill before freezing and thaw in refrigerator.

Doughs *made with gluten-free flours tend to be a touch more sensitive than regular wheat-flour doughs. (For more information on gluten-free flours and doughs, see page 226.) It's important to get to know the brands of flour that you work with. Sometimes you will need to add a bit more liquid, sometimes less. If your dough is a bit sticky, flour your parchment paper with a dusting of sweet rice flour. For kreplach, it doesn't matter if the dough has a little bit of extra flour on top or inside of it. The dough should be pliable without being dry.*

Onion Soup

No need for cheese and bread! This version of onion soup is chockablock full of onions and made all the more flavorful by the addition of silky and mildly sweet rice milk.

Ingredients

3 TBSP	*(heaping)* VEGAN BUTTER
10	LARGE ONIONS, *halved and thinly sliced*
8 CUPS	RICE, SOY, OR ALMOND MILK
4 CUPS	WATER
1 TSP	FRESHLY GROUND BLACK PEPPER
1 TSP	ONION POWDER
1–2 TBSP	*(heaping)* KOSHER SALT

Directions

1 Melt butter in an 8-quart pot set over medium-low heat. Add onions; cook, covered, for 30 minutes or until onions are soft. Add milk, water, and spices to pot. Cover and bring to a boil over high heat.

2 Reduce heat to medium-high. Cook, with lid slightly ajar, for 1 hour.

Freezes very well for up to 6 months. Chill before freezing and thaw in refrigerator.

Rice *milk provides a silky texture for this rich, filling soup.*

Any *kind of onion will work well. Use either plain cooking onions or, for added flavor, try Spanish or Vidalia. When storing onions, keep them as far away as possible from potatoes, as the onions emit a gas that hastens spoilage in potatoes.*

Cream of Broccoli Soup

The perfect savior for those hectic winter days! If you don't have an immersion blender, a regular blender works just as well.

Ingredients

4 LB	BROCCOLI FLORETS
3	LARGE POTATOES, *peeled and cut into quarters*
1–2 TBSP	*(heaping)* KOSHER SALT
1 TSP	*(heaping)* GARLIC POWDER

Directions

1 Place all ingredients into an 8-quart pot. Fill ¾ full with water and bring to a boil over high heat.

2 Reduce heat to medium; cook, with lid slightly ajar, for ½ hour.

3 Remove pot from heat. Place immersion blender in pot; blend until smooth.

Freezes very well for up to 6 months. Chill before freezing and thaw in refrigerator.

If *you look through older cookbooks, you'll find reams of cream soups, all made with 18% or 35% cream. Nowadays, we know that all that high fat cream is a health risk. That doesn't mean we can't still make and enjoy cream soups! Potatoes to the rescue. Adding a potato (or two or three) to your soup, cooking them until tender with either broccoli or cauliflower, and pureeing the mixture ensures a smooth, velvety soup, without a tablespoon of cream in sight!*

Cream of Zucchini Soup

I make this mild soup often, since my family adores it. It's a pale green color so it takes to different garnishes well. For the photo, I chose to garnish it with freshly sliced zucchini, but it also looks lovely with gluten-free croutons or simply served in your favorite china.

Ingredients

5	LARGE ZUCCHINI, *scrubbed clean, washed, and cut into thirds*
3	LARGE POTATOES, *peeled and cut into quarters*
1	LARGE ONION, *halved*
¼ TSP	FRESHLY GROUND BLACK PEPPER
1–2 TBSP	*(heaping)* KOSHER SALT

Directions

1 Place all ingredients into an 8-quart pot. Fill ¾ full with water and bring to a boil over high heat.

2 Reduce heat to medium; cook, with lid slightly ajar, for ½ an hour.

3 Place immersion blender in pot; blend until smooth.

Freezes very well for up to 6 months. Chill before freezing and thaw in refrigerator.

Whether *you call it squash or zucchini, the results are the same—pure delicious. An excellent source of vitamin C, zucchini is available year round but is especially abundant during the late summer months.*

Potato Soup

This satisfying potato soup is almost a meal on its own.

Ingredients

3   LARGE POTATOES, *each cut into about 10 cubes*

2   STALKS CELERY, *sliced*

2   ZUCCHINI, *peeled and sliced*

2   PARSNIPS, *sliced*

2   CARROTS, *sliced*

1 TBSP   KOSHER SALT

Directions

1   Place all ingredients into a 4-quart pot filled almost to the top with water.

2   Cook, covered, over medium heat for 45 minutes.

Store *potatoes in a cool, dry place for up to 2 weeks. (New potatoes should be used within 3 days of purchase.) Warm temperatures can cause a potato to sprout and shrivel. Cold is just as bad. Refrigeration will cause the starch in a potato to convert to sugar, altering its flavor as well as its color once cooked.*

Split Pea Soup with Dumplings

It's amazing how a few basic ingredients can be transformed into something majestic. This easy, nutritious, and completely satisfying soup has been a family favorite for generations.

Ingredients

¼ CUP	OIL
2	ONIONS, *diced*
10	CARROTS, *sliced*
2	MEAT BONES, *optional*
1 PKG	*(16 oz)* GREEN SPLIT PEAS
2 TBSP	*(heaping)* KOSHER SALT

Dumplings

¾ CUP	BROWN RICE FLOUR
¼ CUP	TAPIOCA FLOUR
½ TSP	KOSHER SALT
1 TSP	BAKING POWDER
2 TBSP	OIL
2	LARGE EGGS
2 TBSP	WATER

Directions

1 Heat oil in an 8-quart pot set over medium-high heat. Add onions; cook, stirring, for 5 minutes or until onions are softened.

2 Add carrots and meat bones, if using; sauté for 5 minutes. Add split peas and salt.

3 Fill pot almost to the top with water. Cook, with lid slightly ajar, for 2 hours.

4 Meanwhile, make dumplings. Place rice and tapioca flours, salt, and baking powder in a medium-sized bowl. Stir in oil until absorbed by the dry ingredients. Stir in eggs and water until a batter consistency is formed.

5 Fill a wet or oiled teaspoon half full of batter; drop into boiling soup. Batter should drop easily into soup. If it sticks to spoon, use another wet teaspoon to gently scrape off batter into soup. Repeat with remaining batter, dipping spoon into water as needed.

6 Cook soup for an additional 45 minutes.

Freezes very well for up to 6 months. Chill before freezing and thaw in refrigerator.

Split *peas, like lentils, don't have to be soaked before using, making them more efficient than dried peas, which require an overnight soaking. They're also high in soluble fiber, which helps to bind the bad cholesterol within us and carry it out of the body. Relatively easy on the budget, split peas are also high in protein.*

Vegetable Soup

There are so many wonderful adjectives describe this soup—comforting, nutritious, delicious, filling…

Ingredients

1 PKG	*(16 oz)* GREEN SPLIT PEAS	
1 PKG	*(16 oz)* YELLOW SPLIT PEAS	
2 TBSP	OIL	
2	LARGE ONIONS, *diced*	
7	LARGE CLOVES GARLIC, *crushed*	
5	ZUCCHINI, *diced*	
5	CARROTS, *diced*	
1	LARGE SWEET POTATO, *diced*	
5	STALKS CELERY, *diced*	
3 TBSP	KOSHER SALT	

Directions

1 Place green and yellow split peas in a 6-quart pot. Fill pot ¾ full with water.

2 Bring to a boil over high heat. Reduce heat to medium. Cook, with lid slightly ajar, for 1½ hours.

3 Place immersion blender in pot and blend until smooth.

4 Heat oil in a 12-quart pot set over medium-high heat. Add onions; sauté for 5 minutes or until softened. Stir in garlic. Then stir in zucchini, carrots, sweet potato, celery, and salt. Cook, stirring, for 10 minutes.

5 Stir split pea mixture into vegetables. Pour in enough water to fill ¾ of pot. Rewarm thoroughly over medium heat.

Freezes very well for up to 6 months.

Vegetables *and split peas all together in one pot—this should really be called the Wonder Soup! Split peas are nutritional superstars. They are an excellent source of slow-burning, gluten-free carbohydrates and vegetarian protein, as noted above. But did you know that they are also one of the highest fiber foods you can eat? Cooked slowly with carrots (health warriors too!) and a sweet potato (which outranks most other vegetables in terms of beta-carotene), this colorful soup can't get much healthier.*

Cooking is and should

be a happy adventure. A wonderful sojourn that fills you with a sense of accomplishment and brings contented sighs to those who gather at your table.

Meat and poultry rate high not only in satiety but as complete proteins as well. The components in meat and poultry help with brain function and, due to their protein content, sustain our energy by maintaining consistent blood sugar levels. In addition, most people expect one or the other as a main course at dinner. The recipes in this chapter will take you on a tour of possibilities, keeping you excited about what you're serving your cherished family members.

Marvelous Meat & Poultry

Brisket & Chicken Rollups

This crispy, flavorful recipe is one that I enjoy serving on special occasions.

Ingredients

5	LARGE EGGS
1½ CUPS	POTATO STARCH
½ TSP	KOSHER SALT
¼ TSP	PAPRIKA
2 LB	COOKED OR BAKED BRISKET, *thinly sliced (see French Roast on page 94),* OR 6–8 THIN SLICES PASTRAMI
2 LB	CHICKEN CUTLETS *(or 6 slices), pounded thin and cut into 2-inch strips*
•	OIL, *for frying*

Directions

1. In a bowl, whisk together eggs, potato starch, salt, and paprika with a fork, whisking until a smooth batter forms.

2. Arrange ½ a strip of sliced brisket or pastrami on top of a strip of chicken cutlet. Roll up and secure with a large toothpick or small skewer.

3. Dip rollups into batter until well coated.

4. Heat ½-inch of oil in a large frying pan set over medium-high heat. Fry rollups, without overcrowding pan, until light brown and crisp. Drain on paper towel.

It *may seem curious that this recipe calls for 2 pounds of cooked brisket and only 6 to 8 slices of store-bought pastrami. Isn't 2 pounds of brisket far more than the meager slices of pastrami? It is considerably more, but me and my knife simply can't slice my brisket as thinly as the pastrami is sliced in most stores. Rest assured, regardless of whether you slice a brisket yourself and it ends up on the thicker side or you buy razor-thin slices of pastrami, this dish is manifestly delicious with both.*

Yield *8 to 10 servings*

Cholent is a traditional tasty stew prepared for Shabbos. It is kept warm-hot overnight on a hotplate or in a slow cooker and served at the Shabbos day meal.

Cholent

Ingredients

1 CUP	DRIED RED KIDNEY BEANS
1 CUP	DRIED WHITE NAVY BEANS
3 TBSP	OIL
1	LARGE ONION, *diced*
3	CLOVES GARLIC, *crushed*
1 LB	BEEF STEW OR FLANKEN, OR 2–3 PIECES MINUTE STEAK *(for a lighter version, substitute 1 turkey drumstick or neck)*
2 TBSP	KOSHER SALT
1 TBSP	DRIED MINCED GARLIC
1 TBSP	DRIED MINCED ONION
1 TSP	PAPRIKA
1 TSP	GARLIC POWDER
1 TSP	ONION POWDER
4	POTATOES, *cut in chunks*

Directions

1 Soak beans in lukewarm water overnight or for at least several hours at room temperature. Drain well.

2 Heat oil in an 8-quart pot set over medium-high heat; sauté onions until translucent. Add crushed garlic; sauté for 1 to 2 minutes or until softened.

3 Add meat or turkey to pot; brown for several minutes on each side.

4 Stir in drained beans, minced garlic, minced onion, and spices; reduce heat to medium and simmer for an additional 10 minutes.

5 Stir in potatoes; fill pot ¾ full with water.

6 Cook, covered, over medium heat for 2 to 3 hours or until meat and beans are soft. Cholent may be placed on hotplate overnight.

Dried *beans have hidden in the shadows for so long that people often don't quite know what to do with them or even why they should be eaten. Well, it's time to stock up your pantry with these little gems. They're available all year round and are an economical way to consume protein. In particular, navy and kidney beans are an excellent source of fiber and protein. They're extremely high in calcium and in B vitamins and are a rich source of iron. Both beans have the ability to level blood sugar, a boon for dieters and diabetics alike. Store dried beans in a tightly sealed container in a cool, dry place. Although they won't go bad, the longer you store them, the longer the initial soak will have to be.*

Cornish Hens over Wild Rice

Yield *4 servings*

This dish is in a class by itself; it positively bursts with flavor. It's also beautiful served on a bed of delicious wild rice.

Ingredients

4 Tbsp	OIL
1	LARGE ONION, *finely chopped*
1	SMALL SWEET POTATO, *finely chopped*
2	STALKS CELERY, *finely chopped*
20	CHERRIES, *pitted and halved*
2 tsp	AGAVE OR HONEY
1 tsp	KOSHER SALT
4	CORNISH HENS *(each about 1 lb)*
4 Tbsp	APRICOT JAM

Wild Rice

2 CUPS	WILD RICE
½ CUP	SWEETENED DRIED CRANBERRIES
½ CUP	SLIVERED ALMONDS

Directions

1 Heat oil in a skillet set over medium heat. Add onion; cook, stirring, until translucent. Add sweet potato, celery, cherries, agave, and salt. Cook, stirring, for 30 minutes. The vegetables should still be a bit firm.

2 Preheat oven to 350°.

3 Divide vegetable mixture into 4 equal portions; place inside hollow cavity of Cornish hens. Secure opening with toothpicks; you may need several toothpicks to keep the filling in. It's okay for a bit to come out; it doesn't have to be perfect.

4 Place hens, skin side up, in a 9x13-inch baking pan or glass dish. Cover with parchment paper. Bake for 1½ hours.

5 Remove hens from oven and brush with apricot jam. Return to oven and bake, uncovered, for an additional 10 minutes.

Wild Rice

1 Prepare wild rice according to package instructions.

2 Spread almonds on a parchment-paper–lined baking sheet. Bake in center of a preheated 350° oven, stirring once, for 10 minutes. Add sweetened dried cranberries and toasted almonds to rice before serving.

Wild *rice, despite its name, is not actually a rice at all. Available wild though increasingly cultivated, it is actually a long-grain marsh grass. It is an excellent source of complete protein, containing eight essential amino acids. Wild rice, like all complex carbohydrates, is burned slowly, providing long-lasting energy. It also contains vitamin E, vitamin B, iron, and magnesium.*

Crispy Chicken on Skewers

Yum! Yum! Crushed potato chips and a touch of sweetness, all in one totable package. Kids love this one.

Ingredients

2 LB	CHICKEN CUTLETS *(6 large slices), pounded thin and cut into 2-inch strips*
1 BAG	*(8 oz)* KETTLE-COOKED POTATO CHIPS

Marinade

¾ CUP	MAYONNAISE
2 TBSP	AGAVE OR HONEY
2 TSP	KOSHER SALT
1 TSP	GARLIC POWDER
½ TSP	PAPRIKA
12–15	12-INCH SKEWERS

Directions

1. Preheat oven to 350°.

2. Place skewers in a baking pan filled with cold water to prevent them from splintering.

3. In a small bowl, stir together mayonnaise, agave, salt, garlic powder, and paprika.

4. Crush potato chips either by adding to the bowl of a food processor and pulsing several times until crushed or by placing in a Ziploc bag, squeezing the air out, and rolling a rolling pin over bag. Place crushed chips on a piece of parchment paper. Dip chicken strips into marinade, coating well.

5. Remove skewers from water; pat dry. Thread 1 to 2 chicken strips onto each skewer. Lightly roll chicken skewers in chips, coating well. Suspend skewers along the edges of a 9x13-inch baking pan. Bake in center of oven for 40 minutes.

I shared this recipe as a response to parents coming to me, anxious to get their children to consume more protein. Some children flat out didn't like chicken; for some it was an issue of texture; and for yet others, chicken bones were off-putting. I chose to go with cutlets for the latter reason, eliminating the need to deal with bones. White meat has less texture than dark meat, eliminating that problem as well. Potato chips tend to be a favorite among young diners, so in they went, as did a mild but pleasing mayonnaise-based marinade. The combination was successful, and some parents, once their kids tasted this recipe, have even gone on to add this coating to bone-in chicken.

French Roast

Yield *8 to 10 servings*

You'll enjoy making this French roast when hosting a gourmet meal. It's simple to prepare yet impressive to serve.

Ingredients

½ CUP	EXTRA-VIRGIN OLIVE OIL, *divided*
1	FRENCH ROAST *(about 4 lb)*
1 TBSP	KOSHER SALT
1 TSP	FRESHLY GROUND BLACK PEPPER
1 TSP	DRIED ROSEMARY
½ TSP	PAPRIKA
2 TBSP	DRIED MINCED ONION
2 TBSP	DRIED MINCED GARLIC
1 TSP	ONION POWDER
1 TSP	GARLIC POWDER
1	SMALL PIECE FRESH GINGER, *sliced, optional*
½ CUP	WHITE OR RED SEMIDRY WINE, *optional*
2 TBSP	POTATO STARCH, *dissolved in* 2 TBSP COLD WATER

Directions

1. Rinse the roast and pat it dry. Season with salt, pepper, rosemary, and paprika.

2. Heat 3 Tbsp of oil in a large skillet set over high heat. Add roast; brown on all sides, about 8 minutes.

3. Remove roast from skillet; place on parchment-paper–lined roasting pan. Cool and rub with remaining oil, onion, garlic, onion powder, garlic powder, and fresh ginger, if using. Cover with a sheet of parchment paper, then aluminum foil. Refrigerate for 3 to 6 hours. Remove meat from refrigerator. Pour 2 cups of water and wine, if using, into pan.

4. Recover with parchment paper and aluminum foil. Bake in center of preheated 400° oven for 3 to 4 hours or until a fork glides easily in and out of roast and meat is extremely soft.

5. Reserving sauce, remove meat from pan; let cool. Rewrap meat in parchment paper and foil and refrigerate overnight. Refrigerate sauce as well.

6. While still cold, slice meat against the grain. (Both meat and sauce can be frozen at this point for up to 6 months.)

7. Pour reserved sauce into a 4-quart pot. In a small bowl, stir together potato starch and water. Stir starch into sauce, mixing well. Cook over low heat, stirring occasionally to prevent mixture from sticking to bottom of pot, until heated through and thickened.

8. Pour sauce over meat (either in a roasting pan or a pot). Cook over low heat or warm, covered, in a 350° oven until meat is heated through.

Variation:
*This recipe
works well with
brisket, minute
roast, and
chuck-eye roast.*

Searing *the
meat over high
heat in the skil-
let seals in the
flavors, produc-
ing a tender,
succulent meat
with a perfect
texture. This
is an essential
step to many
meat recipes,
whether you're
making a roast
such as this, a
pot roast, or
even a simple
steak on the
grill.*

Grilled Chicken Cutlets

Grilling is the perfect choice when a light, quick dinner is on the menu.

Ingredients

2 LB	CHICKEN CUTLETS *(6 large slices), pounded thin*

Marinade

¼ CUP	NEUTRAL FLAVORED OIL
2 TBSP	EXTRA-VIRGIN OLIVE OIL
6	CLOVES GARLIC, *crushed*
1 TSP	KOSHER SALT
1 TBSP	*(heaping)* DRIED PARSLEY LEAVES

Directions

1 In a bowl, stir together marinade ingredients; add cutlets, turning until well coated. Cover and marinade in refrigerator for at least 30 minutes or for up to 4 hours. Preheat grill pan set over high heat for 5 minutes.

2 Remove chicken from marinade; discard marinade. Place chicken on grill; cook until it turns white, 2 to 4 minutes. Turn chicken over; cook for an additional 2 to 4 minutes or until cooked through.

This *is a basic marinade, delicious on its own, but also wonderful as a canvas on which to layer other flavors. Try whisking in 2 Tbsp balsamic vinegar along with 1 Tbsp Dijon mustard. When fresh herbs are available, chop up some fresh basil, along with parsley and dill or mint, for a refreshing change of pace. If citrus is more to your liking, add the juice of half a lemon as well as a touch of honey.*

Grilled Patties

A light, pleasant choice for the summer months.

Ingredients

1½ LB	GROUND DARK CHICKEN
1½ LB	GROUND DARK TURKEY
2	POTATOES, *peeled, cooked, and mashed well*
2	LARGE ONIONS, *finely diced and sautéed*
3	LARGE EGGS
2 TSP	KOSHER SALT
2 TSP	GARLIC POWDER
½ TSP	PAPRIKA
¼ TSP	FRESHLY GROUND BLACK PEPPER

Directions

1 In a large bowl, mix together ground chicken and turkey, mashed potatoes, sautéed onions, eggs, and spices. Form into 30 to 35 small patties.

2 Preheat a grill pan set over high heat for 5 minutes.

3 In batches, place patties on grill; cook, turning once, for about 4 minutes or until no longer pink inside.

When *making grilled chicken patties, opt for dark ground chicken. It results in a juicier patty than white meat only. I have also made this recipe with ⅓ dark ground chicken, ⅓ dark ground turkey, and ⅓ ground veal, which is incredibly delicious. This recipe also works like magic as a meatloaf. The mixture can be frozen as a block to turn into patties or a meatloaf at a later date. Or freeze as patties to be grilled later, so you'll never be without a dinner at the ready.*

Honey-Glazed Chicken

Yield *4 servings*

As this chapter was being reviewed, my editor asked me what chicken bottoms were. I didn't know what else to call them, but together we figured out that I was referring to whole chicken legs. Call them bottoms or legs, the end result is pure delicious.

Ingredients

4	CHICKEN BOTTOMS OR WHOLE CHICKEN LEGS

Marinade

2 TBSP	MAYONNAISE
1 TBSP	HONEY OR AGAVE
½ TSP	KOSHER SALT
¼ TSP	GARLIC POWDER
¼ TSP	MUSTARD POWDER

Directions

1. Fold a piece of parchment paper in half and place on top of countertop grill set over high heat. (I like to use the George Foreman grill, which has only one setting.) Place chicken directly on top of parchment paper; grill for 40 minutes.

2. Meanwhile, stir together marinade ingredients in a small plate or bowl.

3. Spread marinade on chicken pieces; grill for an additional 10 minutes.

You've *heard of the old adage "Err on the side of caution." Well, in kitchens across the world, the saying should be phrased, "Err on the side of safety!" When buying chicken, try to get home as soon as possible so that you can get your poultry into the cool climes of your refrigerator. If you bought your chicken frozen and then thawed it, do not refreeze it again until it's fully cooked. Chicken should always be cooked to an internal temperature of 165°F.*

Sautéed Liver

Yield *4 servings*

Although simple, this liver dish is delicious. I still can't believe how many "wow" reviews it received.

Ingredients

½ CUP	OIL
2	LARGE ONIONS, *diced*
½ LB	BROILED CHICKEN LIVER, *cut in bite-size pieces*
2 TBSP	AGAVE OR HONEY
1 TSP	KOSHER SALT
½ TSP	GARLIC POWDER
½ TSP	PAPRIKA
¼ TSP	DRIED MINCED GARLIC
¼ TSP	DRIED MINCED ONION
⅛ TSP	FRESHLY GROUND BLACK PEPPER

Directions

1. Heat oil in a skillet set over medium-high heat. Add onions; cook, stirring, until golden.

2. Add liver, agave, and spices to skillet. Reduce heat to low; cover and cook, stirring, for 30 minutes. Uncover pot; cook for an additional 10 to 15 minutes or until liver is crisp.

3. This dish is best served within 3 days.

Liver *is a rich source of iron. Iron oxygenates our blood, which allows nutrients to circulate more freely and invigorates our energy levels. This is true of both chicken and beef liver. However, beef liver is higher in iron.*

Meatballs & Spaghetti in Tomato Sauce

Yield *8 servings*

Here's a dish to please all ages—children's favorite meatballs in a yummy tomato sauce with the added bonus ingredient of flanken for more adult tastes. Use the home-made tomato sauce on the next page for a lighter, tastier version.

Ingredients

1 BAG	*(16 oz)* BROWN RICE SPAGHETTI

Tomato Sauce

3 TBSP	OIL
1	LARGE ONION, *finely diced*
2	STRIPS BONE-IN FLANKEN
1 CAN	*(15 oz)* TOMATO JUICE
½ CUP	AGAVE, XYLITOL, OR SUGAR
½ TSP	KOSHER SALT
¼ TSP	FRESHLY GROUND BLACK PEPPER

Meatballs

½ CUP	UNCOOKED WHITE RICE
3 TBSP	OIL
1	LARGE ONION, *finely diced*
3	CLOVES GARLIC, *crushed*
2 LB	GROUND CHICKEN, MEAT, OR TURKEY *(a combination is best)*
3	LARGE EGGS
½ TSP	KOSHER SALT
½ CUP	SELTZER OR WATER

One of the keys to making wonderful meatballs (and hamburgers and meatloaf, for that matter) is to be very gentle with your meat mixture. Overmixing and overhandling tends to result in a tougher meatball. I added rice for a softer consistency.

Directions

Tomato Sauce

1. Heat oil in an 8-quart pot set over medium-high heat. Add onion; sauté until translucent. Add flanken; brown for several minutes on each side.

2. Add remaining sauce ingredients and 6 cups water. Bring to a boil; reduce heat to medium and cook, covered, for 30 minutes.

3. Meanwhile, make meatball mixture. (See instructions opposite.)

4. Form walnut-size balls of the meatball mixture and drop into simmering sauce. This recipe will yield about 2 dozen meatballs. Cook, covered, for 1 hour.

5. Prepare spaghetti according to package instructions and serve topped with meatballs and sauce.

Meatballs

1. In a 4-quart pot, bring ½ cup water to a boil. Add rice; reduce heat and simmer, covered, for 16 to 18 minutes or until rice is tender and water evaporates.

2. Heat oil in a small skillet set over medium heat and sauté onion and garlic for 10 to 15 minutes or until very soft.

3. In a large bowl, mix together onions, garlic, cooked rice, ground chicken, eggs, salt, and seltzer, mixing until a firm mixture is formed.

Homemade Tomato Sauce

Yield **Enough for 2 dozen meatballs**

You reap all sorts of rewards when you make homemade tomato sauce. Not only do you know exactly what you put into it, but it's also lighter, less sweet, and certainly contains less sodium.

Ingredients

18	VINE-RIPENED TOMATOES
3 Tbsp	EXTRA-VIRGIN OLIVE OIL
1	LARGE ONION, *finely diced*
1	CLOVE GARLIC, *minced*
1	RED PEPPER, *thinly sliced lengthwise*
½ cup	AGAVE, XYLITOL, OR GRANULATED SUGAR
2 Tbsp	KOSHER SALT
2 tsp	GARLIC POWDER
2 tsp	ONION POWDER

Directions

1. In an 8-quart pot, bring 8 cups water to a rolling boil.

2. Carefully add 9 of the tomatoes to boiling water; cook for 3 minutes. The peel will begin to crack open and the skin will soften, but the insides will remain firm. Remove tomatoes with a slotted spoon; place into a large bowl.

3. Place remaining 9 tomatoes in boiling water for 3 minutes. Remove with a slotted spoon and place with the other 9 tomatoes in the bowl. Cool slightly. Using both hands, squeeze tomatoes a bit to make them mushy.

4. Wash and dry the 8-quart pot. Add oil to pot and heat over medium-high heat. Add onion; sauté until translucent. Add garlic and red pepper; sauté for 4 minutes. Add tomatoes and all juices to pot; bring to a boil. Reduce heat to low; cook, covered, for 30 minutes.

5. Remove pot from heat. Place immersion blender directly into pot; blend until smooth and saucy. Stir in agave and spices. Return to heat; bring to a rolling boil. Reduce heat to medium and add meatballs.

Freezes well for up to 6 months.

Quinoa

Yield *4 to 5 servings*

Quinoa, the grain with the most protein, is wonderful on its own but is even more tempting prepared in the colorful, flavorful manner described below.

This *recipe works wonderfully well as a bed for the Meatballs in Pepper Sauce, equally well as a side dish to accompany the meatballs, and is a delightful accompaniment to any main dish. For that matter, it's an amazing, award-winning vegetarian dish.*

It's *so interesting how foods go in and out of favor. When I started developing recipes for this collection, I was worried that calling for quinoa might be troublesome. After all, you have to rinse it, you have to cook it, its texture is a bit chewy. Quite frankly, I just wasn't sure how my readers would take to it. How wrong I was! Now quinoa recipes are ubiquitous, and I do believe that it is a hearty grain that is here to stay.*

Directions

1 Place quinoa in a sieve; rinse under cold running water until water runs clear. This step removes the bitter coating. Drain well.

2 Place quinoa in a 6-quart pot. Add 2 cups water. Season with salt; bring to a rolling boil. Reduce heat to medium-low; cook for 15 to 20 minutes or until water has evaporated and quinoa is fluffy. Fluff with a fork.

3 Heat oil in a large skillet set over medium heat; add garlic, cook for 1 minute. Stir in carrots, celery, and parsley; cook, stirring, for 5 minutes, no longer.

4 Add quinoa and lemon juice.

5 Fluff with a fork and serve.

Ingredients

1 CUP	QUINOA
¼ TSP	KOSHER SALT
3 TBSP	EXTRA-VIRGIN OLIVE OIL
1–2	CLOVES GARLIC, *crushed*
½ CUP	FINELY DICED CARROTS *(1 small carrot)*
½ CUP	FINELY DICED CELERY *(2 stalks)*
½ CUP	FINELY CHOPPED FRESH PARSLEY *(or 1 Tbsp dried parsley)*
¼ CUP	FRESHLY SQUEEZED LEMON JUICE

Meatballs in Pepper Sauce with Quinoa

Tomato allergy? There's no need to feel deprived. This recipe, so close in flavor and taste to the real deal, was created with lots of heart, just for you.

Ingredients

- MEATBALLS
  (see page 104)

- QUINOA
  (see page 107)

Pepper Sauce

5 TBSP	EXTRA-VIRGIN OLIVE OIL
1	LARGE ONION, *diced*
6	LARGE RED PEPPERS, *thinly sliced lengthwise*
1	CLOVE GARLIC
1–2	BAY LEAVES
1 TBSP	AGAVE, XYLITOL, OR GRANULATED SUGAR
1 TBSP	KOSHER SALT

Directions

1. Heat 3 Tbsp of the oil in an 8-quart pot set over medium-high heat. Add half of the onion; sauté until translucent. Add peppers and garlic; reduce heat to medium-low and cook, covered, for 10 to 12 minutes or until soft.

2. Transfer mixture to a blender; add 3 cups of water. Blend until pureed. (If you need to divide the blending process in two shifts, divide the water in half as well.) Pour pureed vegetables into a large bowl.

3. Wash and dry the 8-quart pot. Add remaining oil to pot and heat over medium-high heat. Add remaining onion; sauté for 3 minutes. Add pureed peppers, 5 cups water, bay leaves, sweetener, and salt. Reduce heat to low; cook, covered, for 30 minutes.

4. Bring pepper sauce to a rolling boil once again. Form walnut-size balls of the meatball mixture and place in the sauce. Reduce heat to medium; cook, covered for 1 hour. Remove bay leaves before serving. Serve over quinoa.

This *is a wonderful alternative to tomato sauce and can be used anywhere you might use a classic tomato-based sauce. Use for a shakshouka, a chicken paprikash, or even stirred into a risotto. Like tomato sauce, it also freezes beautifully, for up to 6 months. Be sure to buy heavy, plump red peppers for this sauce. Red peppers should be stored in the fridge, where they will keep for up to 5 days.*

Chicken à la Chasseur

This dish was inspired by Chicken Marsala. I've stayed true to the original inspiration but made it gluten-free with the substitution of potato starch.

Ingredients

1½ LB	CHICKEN CUTLETS *(4 large slices), pounded thin*
½ CUP	POTATO STARCH
4 TBSP	OIL, *divided*
1 BOX	*(8–10 oz)* FRESH MUSHROOMS *(buttons or stuffers)*
1	LARGE ONION, *diced*
½ CUP	SEMIDRY RED WINE
1½ TSP	KOSHER SALT
¼ TSP	FRESHLY GROUND PEPPER
½ TSP	DRIED OREGANO, *optional*

Directions

1. Coat chicken in potato starch. Heat half of oil in a skillet set over medium heat. Cook chicken, in batches if necessary, until golden, about 2 minutes on each side. Remove chicken from skillet.

2. Peel mushroom caps if desired. Remove stems; slice thinly.

3. Heat remaining oil in skillet. Add onion; sauté until translucent. Add mushrooms to skillet; sauté for 5 minutes. Stir in wine, salt, pepper, and oregano, if using. Increase heat to medium-high; cook for 5 minutes. Pour in 2 cups water; bring to a rolling boil.

4. Return chicken to skillet; cook, covered, for 8 minutes.

Did you know that mushrooms are like little sponges? If you submerge them in water to clean, they will absorb a lot of that water. Then, when you're cooking them, they will take longer to cook, since they have to release all of that excess water, which then has to evaporate. The trick to cleaning them is to rub a damp cloth all around their surface to remove any dirt. Alternatively, you can peel away the thin outer layer.

One-Pot Turkey Meal

A wonderful dish full of comfort and satisfaction for the cold winter months.

Ingredients

2 TBSP	OIL
1	LARGE ONION, *diced*
1½ LB	TURKEY STEWING MEAT
1 TBSP	KOSHER SALT
¾ TSP	PAPRIKA
1 TSP	AGAVE, XYLITOL, OR GRANULATED SUGAR
3	LARGE POTATOES OR 2 LARGE POTATOES AND 1 SWEET POTATO, *peeled and cubed*

Directions

1 Heat oil in a 6-quart pot set over medium heat. Add onion; sauté until translucent. Add turkey, salt, paprika, and agave; stir for 2 to 3 minutes until meat is well coated with onions and spices.

2 Add 3 cups of water; cook, covered, for 1 hour. Stir in potatoes, adding more water to ensure that potatoes are covered with water. Cook for 30 to 45 minutes or until meat and potatoes are tender.

Remarkable *roots!! Hidden away underground, these vegetables are a treasure trove of minerals and nutrients, not to mention taste. Although this stew is great with potatoes, feel free to mix things up a bit and use peeled and cubed parsnips or turnips instead. They are a bit sweeter than potatoes, but the turkey meat can handle it. Or use peeled, chopped carrots and turnips. Just try to avoid using sweet potatoes with parsnips, as the stew may come out too sweet.*

Pepper Steak

This particular version of pepper steak is light and tasty while still being incredibly tender.

Ingredients

3 Tbsp	EXTRA-VIRGIN OLIVE OIL
1	LARGE ONION, *sliced*
1	RED PEPPER, *thinly sliced lengthwise*
1	GREEN PEPPER, *thinly sliced lengthwise*
1	YELLOW PEPPER, *thinly sliced lengthwise*
1 LB	PEPPER STEAK
1 TSP	KOSHER SALT
¼ TSP	PAPRIKA
⅛ TSP	FRESHLY GROUND BLACK PEPPER

Directions

1. Heat oil in a large saucepan set over medium heat. Add onion; sauté until translucent. Add peppers; sauté for 5 to 10 minutes or until softened. Push onions and peppers to one side of saucepan.

2. Place pepper steak in saucepan. Increase heat to high; brown steak for 2 to 3 minutes on each side. Add spices and 2 cups water. Bring to a rolling boil. Reduce heat to medium-low; cook, covered, for 1 to 1½ hours or until meat is tender.

Although *this colorful dish is delicious accompanied by rice, pasta, or mashed potatoes, there's a world of pureed vegetables that can do the trick as well. Try using sweet potatoes instead of Idaho when making mashed potatoes. Cauliflower, when pureed, makes a delicious mock mashed potato. Even parsnips and turnips are incredibly tasty when cooked and then pureed, either to a coarse consistency or to a velvety smoothness.*

Homemade Schwarma

Yield **3 to 4 servings**

A homemade version of a popular Middle Eastern dish that's quick, easy, and superbly spiced!

Ingredients

1–1½ LB	CHICKEN CUTLETS, *pounded thin and cut into nuggets*

Marinade

2 TSP	OIL
1 TBSP	VINEGAR
1 TSP	GARLIC POWDER
1 TSP	KOSHER SALT
1 TSP	PAPRIKA
1 TSP	GROUND CUMIN
1 TSP	ONION POWDER
1 TSP	FRESHLY GROUNDED BLACK PEPPER

Directions

1 In a large bowl, stir together marinade ingredients. Add chicken nuggets, turning to coat well. Cover and refrigerate for at least 30 minutes or for up to 8 hours.

2 Spray large skillet set over high heat. Cook chicken, in batches if necessary, for 4 to 5 minutes per side or until no longer pink inside.

This *is a great dish with which to be creative. Serve in warmed pitas or lafas. Have small bowls of tahini and hummus (see pages 28–29) on your table as well as heaps of sliced raw vegetables. Let your family choreograph their very own personalized schwarma.*

Variation: *Want the spice, but not that spicy? Cut the cumin and black pepper to ½ tsp.*

Shoulder Steak

Just four words are required to describe this tantalizing dish: savory, succulent, easy, and elegant!

Ingredients

¼ CUP	OIL
3	CLOVES GARLIC, *minced*
3	LARGE ONIONS, *sliced thinly*
1 LB	SHOULDER STEAK OR PEPPER STEAK OR 4 PIECES MINUTE STEAK
1 CUP	SEMIDRY RED WINE
1	BAY LEAF
1 TSP	KOSHER SALT
½ TSP	DRIED MINCED GARLIC
¼ TSP	DRIED ROSEMARY LEAVES, *optional*
⅛ TSP	FRESHLY GROUND PEPPER

Directions

1 Heat oil in a large skillet set over medium heat. Add garlic; brown for about 1 minute. Add onions; sauté until translucent, 3 to 5 minutes.

2 Add steak, wine, bay leaf, and spices. Increase heat to high; bring to a boil. Add 5 cups water; return to a boil. Reduce heat to medium; cook, covered, for 2 to 2½ hours or until meat is tender. Remove bay leaf before serving.

Freezes well for up to 6 months.

Shoulder *steak is one of those meats that takes exceptionally well to braising. Because it has so little fat, it can be a tough cut, but the good news is that it's chockfull of flavor. Braising, which means cooking gently and slowly in liquid, helps coax out all that natural flavor while also ensuring the inherent toughness gently gets transformed into a tender, melt-in-the-mouth goodness.*

Spiced Baked Chicken

A tasty twist to baked chicken that remains quick and easy to prepare and is enjoyed by adults and children alike.

Ingredients

4	WHOLE CHICKEN LEGS OR BOTTOMS *(or 1 chicken cut in quarters)*

Marinade

⅓ CUP	EXTRA-VIRGIN OLIVE OIL
2 Tbsp	DRIED MINCED ONION
2 Tbsp	DRIED MINCED GARLIC
1 TSP	ONION POWDER
1 TSP	GARLIC POWDER
1 TSP	KOSHER SALT
½ TSP	PAPRIKA
⅛ TSP	FRESHLY GROUND BLACK PEPPER

Directions

1. In bowl, stir together marinade ingredients.

2. Place chicken in a parchment-paper–lined 9x13-inch baking foil pan or glass dish. Pour marinade over chicken. Cover and refrigerate for at least 3 hours or overnight.

3. Bake, covered, in a pre-heated 350° oven for 2½ hours. Uncover; bake for 30 minutes or until crispy.

Tip: *For an equally convenient and tasty side dish, peel and cube 4 to 5 potatoes (you can use a mix of regular and sweet potatoes). Add to chicken and bake covered in a 350° oven for 3 hours, then uncover and cook for ½ hour.*

Marinades, *as every cook knows, are a tried-and-true method of adding a menuful of flavor to meats. They help make meats and poultry tenderer by either coating with a protective barrier such as the oil found here or by including an acid. The presence of an acid starts the cooking process way before the meat hits any heat, breaking down any tough sinews. In this recipe, the marinade seals in all of the chicken's natural moistness and flavor, ensuring a wonderfully juicy chicken each and every time.*

Grilled Stuffed Peppers

This dish elevates stuffed peppers to a whole new sphere of delicious. Inspired by a Mexican delicacy, these peppers are not only stuffed but also dipped in a special batter and fried for an exquisite taste sensation.

Ingredients

10	RED PEPPERS *(or color of your choice)*

Filling

2 TBSP	OIL
2	ONIONS, *diced*
1	RED PEPPER, *diced*
1 LB	GROUND CHICKEN OR BEEF
2	POTATOES, *peeled, diced, and cooked*
2 TSP	KOSHER SALT
½ TSP	PAPRIKA
¼ TSP	FRESHLY GROUND BLACK PEPPER

Coating

5	LARGE EGGS
½ CUP	OIL
2½ CUPS	POTATO STARCH

Directions

1. Preheat grill pan for 3 minutes over high heat. Reduce heat to medium-high. In batches, grill peppers, turning, for 15 to 20 minutes or until blackened on all sides and softened. Remove peppers from heat; transfer to large bowl. Cover bowl with plastic wrap for 15 minutes. This will help retain moisture, making it easier to peel away the skin. Using a small sharp paring knife, peel away charred skin.

2. Cut off top and slice open one side to hollow out pepper.

Filling

1. Heat oil in skillet set over medium heat. Add onions; sauté until translucent. Add diced pepper; sauté for 3 minutes.

2. Add ground chicken or meat. Cook, stirring constantly, for 10 minutes or until no longer pink inside. Stir in potatoes, salt, paprika, and pepper, mixing well. Spoon filling evenly into peppers.

Coating

1. Separate eggs. Transfer egg whites to the bowl of an electric mixer fitted with whisk attachment. Beat until whites are the consistency of snow. Add egg yolks to whites; whisk gently for 1 minute or until combined.

2. Heat oil in a large sauté pan set over medium-high heat.

3. Dip stuffed peppers into potato starch until sides are well coated. Dip each pepper into egg mixture. Add peppers to hot oil, in batches if necessary, and fry for 2 to 3 minutes per side or until golden.

I cut open the peppers to ensure that all of the laws of kashruth were followed. That meant I had to be quite gentle when filling, dipping, and frying the peppers. But it can be done. I donned a pair of latex gloves, held the cut side to prevent any of the filling from spilling out, and dipped the entire pepper into the starch and then the egg whites. It's important to coat them well so that a seal is created, yet another way of keeping the filling where it should be. Use tongs or two slotted spoons to ease the peppers into the hot oil, with the cut side up or at least on the side.

Full of good-for-you

fats and the star of those fats, omega-3, fish is worth investing in more often. Whether you choose a meatier fish such as salmon or some-thing delicate like sole, you're doing your heart and body a world of good. For fish buying know-how, see the tip on page 130.

Fabulous Fish

Baked Salmon in Marinade

Yield *4 to 6 salmon servings*

This fish is our Shabbos specialty. Because of its simplicity, you'll love it too. I have been making my gefilte fish this way for a long time. It infuses the gefilte fish with an unparalleled flavor.

Ingredients

4–6	SMALL 1-INCH SALMON FILLETS
1	ROLL GEFILTE FISH, *optional*
1 CUP	AGAVE, XYLITOL, OR GRANULATED SUGAR
4 Tbsp	FRESHLY SQUEEZED LEMON JUICE
1 Tbsp	VINEGAR
1½ TSP	KOSHER SALT
½ TSP	GROUND ALLSPICE OR 2 Tbsp WHOLE ALLSPICE
8	BAY LEAVES

Directions

1 Preheat oven to 425°.

2 Place salmon, skin side up, and gefilte fish, if using, in a 10x14-inch heavy-duty aluminum pan lined with parchment paper.

3 In a bowl, combine sweetener, lemon juice, vinegar, kosher salt, allspice, and bay leaves with 2 cups water. Pour over fish.

4 Bake, covered, in center of preheated oven for 1 hour. Reduce heat to 350°. Uncover fish and bake for an additional 30 minutes.

5 Discard bay leaves. Cool fish slightly in liquid. Remove outer paper from gefilte fish roll. Cover pan and refrigerate overnight. Bring to room temperature before serving.

Tip: *For a golden and slightly crispy finish, place fish skin-side down and use agave as your sweetener.*

To *achieve a sauce clear of any minute speckles that may appear as a result of the ground allspice, you can strain the sauce immediately after baking the fish and then spoon it over the fish once again.*

Salmon *is a wonderful delicious way to increase your intake of omega-3 fatty acids. In fact, in the wide world of fish, salmon has among the highest levels of omega-3's. These essential fatty acids perform a multitude of beneficial chores: they help reduce inflammation, thereby minimizing joint pain; they optimize brain health; and they even protect our skin. For an extra hit of omega-3's, try a handful of walnuts during the day, as walnuts are known for their unusually high omega-3 content.*

Gefilte Fish

A taste of home! Make your own gefilte fish in honor of Shabbos.

Ingredients

Gefilte Roll

1½ LB	GROUND WHITE FISH
2	LARGE EGGS
¼ CUP	AGAVE OR GRANULATED SUGAR
1	ONION, *grated (or 1 tsp onion powder)*
1 TBSP	KOSHER SALT
⅛ TSP	FRESHLY GROUND BLACK PEPPER

Cooking Liquid

2	LARGE ONIONS
3	CARROTS, *peeled and sliced into circles*
1 TBSP	KOSHER SALT
¼ CUP	AGAVE, XYLITOL, OR GRANULATED SUGAR

Directions

1. Place fish, eggs, agave, and grated onion in the bowl of an electric mixer. Mix on high speed for 10 minutes. Add salt and pepper and mix another minute.

2. Moisten a piece of parchment paper under cold running water. Place half of fish mixture into center of parchment paper. Form into a roll, tucking in paper at each end. Repeat with remaining fish. Freeze both logs for 6 to 8 hours or until firm enough to retain their shape.

3. To cook, place onions, carrots, and salt in an 8-quart pot filled ⅔ of the way with water.

4. Bring water to a boil. Add fish rolls; reduce heat to low.

5. Cook, covered, for 2 hours. Cool fish slightly in liquid. Remove outer paper from rolls. Transfer rolls to a glass dish along with liquid and carrots. Cover dish and refrigerate overnight. Bring to room temperature before slicing and serving.

Tip: *Today, gluten-free ready-made gefilte fish can be found in many stores and supermarkets. Simply follow the cooking directions above or bake with your salmon, as in the preceding recipe.*

For *a dense-textured roll that most closely resembles a store-bought variety, it's important to mix the fish for the required 10 minutes. If you mix it with a spoon or for a shorter period of time, your gefilte fish will be softer in texture and more patty-like.*

Baked Sole

Sole, like most fish, is a fabulous way to enjoy a lean protein.

Ingredients

4	SOLE FILLETS
1 TBSP	FRESHLY SQUEEZED LEMON JUICE
3 TBSP	MAYONNAISE
1 TSP	KOSHER SALT
½ TSP	GARLIC POWDER
⅛ TSP	FRESHLY GROUND BLACK PEPPER

Directions

1 Preheat oven to 350°.

2 Rinse sole and pat dry. Place fish in a parchment-paper–lined 9x13-inch baking pan.

3 Pour lemon juice over fish.

4 In a small bowl, combine mayonnaise and spices and smear on both sides of fish.

5 Bake, covered, in center of preheated oven for 15 to 20 minutes or until fish is softened and flakes easily with a fork.

When *purchasing fresh fish (for example, salmon, sole, tilapia, or halibut), always look for flesh that is moist and translucent. Regardless of whether you are buying fillets or a whole fish, it should have a sweet, fresh scent and never smell "fishy." Depending on whether or not you're going to use it right away, inquire as to whether the fish has been previously frozen. If it has already been thawed, then you know you should use it right away. Always cook fish within a day or two of purchase.*

Eggplant & Sole Envelopes

Yield *20 pieces*

This elegant entrée is sure to please even the "skip the fish" people in your home. The high oil content allows your eggplant and fish to be buttery soft.

Ingredients

2	LARGE EGGPLANTS, *sliced lengthwise, for a total of 20 slices*
2 TBSP	KOSHER SALT
5	SOLE FILLETS, *cut into 20 equal-sized squares*
1½ CUPS	POTATO STARCH
1 CUP	OIL

Mushroom Sauce

2 TBSP	OIL
1	LARGE ONION, *diced*
1 BOX	*(8–10 oz)* FRESH MUSHROOMS *(buttons or stuffers), stemmed and sliced*
2 TSP	SALT
¼ TSP	PAPRIKA
⅛ TSP	FRESHLY GROUND PEPPER
1 TBSP	POTATO STARCH
1½ CUPS	COLD WATER
1 CUP	SELTZER

Directions

1. Place eggplant on a foil-lined baking sheet and sprinkle liberally with salt. Let stand at room temperature for 30 minutes to allow the bitterness to be extracted.

2. Gently squeeze eggplant, 5 to 10 slices at a time, to remove any excess water.

3. Place potato starch in a bowl for coating.

4. Place 1 piece of sole in the center of 1 slice of eggplant. Fold right side to the center and then fold left side to the center. Repeat with remaining sole and eggplant slices. Coat sole and eggplant envelopes in potato starch.

5. Heat oil in a large skillet set over low heat. In batches, cook eggplant envelopes for 8 to 10 minutes or until slightly golden.

Mushroom Sauce

1. Heat oil in a skillet set over medium-high heat. Add onion; sauté until translucent. Add mushrooms and spices to onions. Sauté for 30 minutes.

2. Dissolve potato starch in water and seltzer. Stir into mushroom mixture. Cook, stirring, until thickened, adding more water to obtain desired consistency.

3. Serve over sole and eggplant envelopes.

Typically, mushroom sauces are thickened with cornstarch, which lends them a silky consistency. To avoid using a corn-based product, I tried potato starch instead. At first, I was disappointed with the results, since the sauce didn't have that luxurious smooth-ness. Then I tried dissolving the potato starch in both regular water and seltzer, and the sauce came out exactly as I had imagined. Smooth, silky, and delicious. I'm not sure why the seltzer made all the difference, but it did, and that's why it's in this recipe.

It's so simple and economical to make your own healthy and tasty version of this classic appetizer.

Herring

Ingredients

Herring I

3	STRIPS MATJES HERRING, *cut into bite-size pieces*
⅓ CUP	OIL
1	ONION, *diced*
2	LOX SLICES, *cut in bite-size pieces, optional*

Herring II

3	STRIPS CREAM HERRING, *cut into bite-size pieces*
3 TBSP	MAYONNAISE
1 TSP	VINEGAR
1 TBSP	XYLITOL OR GRANULATED SUGAR
1	ONION, *diced*
1 TSP	WHOLE ALLSPICE

Directions

For Both Recipes

- In a bowl or container, mix all ingredients together. Marinate overnight in the refrigerator for best results.

It's *funny how a decade or two can change the way we look at a certain food. Not so long ago, herring was a no-no, due to its perceived high fat content. We now know that herring is blessed with heart-healthy fat, and it has regained its rightful place in the arena of good health.*

I have found that

people who embark on a gluten- and dairy-free journey sometimes bemoan the anticipated loss of personal favorites. They worry that they'll have to give up their favorite pancake recipe or piece of cheesecake. Sometimes it's a question of missing certain textures as much as the perceived loss of a favorite dish. This is why I was so excited when I stared developing recipes for this section and why I felt it was so crucial to include this chapter.

Milk alternatives as well as those for sour cream and cream cheese have come a long way in replicating the smooth, silky sensation typically associated with the real dairy item. The recipes on the following pages can be created with any of the three milk substitutes listed, namely rice, almond, or soy.

Magnificent Mock Dairy

Mock Cheese Blintzes

A delicious delight as an entrée, side, or main dish. Your family will find it difficult to believe that this rich, flavorful blintz is not dairy.

Ingredients

Crepes

⅔ CUP	BROWN RICE FLOUR
⅓ CUP	TAPIOCA FLOUR
¼ CUP	POTATO STARCH
1 TSP	XANTHAN GUM
10	LARGE EGGS
1 CUP	RICE, ALMOND, OR SOY MILK
½ CUP	WATER
½ CUP	XYLITOL OR GRANULATED SUGAR
1 TSP	OIL
¼ TSP	VANILLA EXTRACT
•	OIL, *for frying*

Filling

2	CONTAINERS *(8 oz each)* TOFU CREAM CHEESE, *softened*
½ CUP	XYLITOL OR GRANULATED SUGAR
4 TBSP	VEGAN SOUR CREAM
DASH	VANILLA EXTRACT
•	SPRINKLE CINNAMON

Directions

Crepes

1. In a bowl, stir together rice and tapioca flours, potato starch, and xanthan gum. Set aside.

2. In the bowl of an electric mixer or a food processor, beat together eggs, milk, water, xylitol, oil, and vanilla. Add dry ingredients, mixing until well blended.

3. Heat a skillet set over medium heat; spray or dab with a bit of oil. Using a soup ladle or approximately 3 to 4 Tbsp of batter, pour batter into hot pan, tilting and rotating pan so that it is evenly coated with batter. Cook on one side until lightly golden and the sides of the crepe start to separate from the pan. Flip crepe; cook until golden. As the crepes are finished, layer between sheets of waxed paper.

Filling

- In a bowl, mix together cream cheese, xylitol, sour cream, vanilla, and cinnamon.

Assembly

1. Place 1½ to 2 Tbsp of filling in center of each crepe. Fold sides a bit to center, partially covering filling. Starting from the bottom, roll crepe up completely.

2. You may also simply roll blintzes without folding in the sides.

3. Serve with a dollop of sour cream or strawberry sauce. (See page 146.)

   These blintzes freeze very well for up to 6 months.

Variation: *For a petite blintz, use a small frying pan. Try it, it makes a statement!*

Tip: *If you are using xylitol in the filling, make sure that the cream cheese is at room temperature. This allows the xylitol crystals to fully dissolve.*

I *always thought that blintzes had to be a one-day affair. But no more. If you're pressed for time, simply wrap the plate of freshly made crepes with plastic wrap and refrigerate for up to one day. They will be as pliable as if they just came out of the frying pan.*

Layered Potatoes & Eggs

Yield *4 to 6 servings*

A Hungarian classic that never goes out of fashion. It's packed with protein and is enriched by the addition of butter. The potatoes cook down to a tender-yet-crisp consistency, bathed as they are in the smooth sour cream.

Ingredients

6	LARGE POTATOES
3 TBSP	VEGAN BUTTER
9	HARD-BOILED EGGS
•	KOSHER SALT, *to taste*
1	CONTAINER *(12 oz)* VEGAN SOUR CREAM

Directions

1 Wash potatoes, scrubbing until clean. Place in a pot of water. Bring to a boil; cook until tender, about 30 minutes. Let cool slightly. Peel and slice potatoes. Slice eggs in circles.

2 In a large skillet set over medium heat, melt butter. Remove skillet from heat. Arrange a single layer of sliced potatoes in skillet. Sprinkle with salt. Arrange a single layer of sliced eggs on top of potatoes. Sprinkle with salt. Spread half of sour cream over eggs. Repeat layering, ending with potatoes. Top with remaining sour cream.

3 Set skillet over medium-low heat. Cook, covered, for 30 minutes.

Variation: *For a lighter version, use 3 Tbsp sour cream only on top.*

You *can bake this dish, covered, in a preheated 375° oven for 30 minutes. Uncover for an additional 5 to 10 minutes to achieve a crispy finish.*

Eggs *are one of those perfect foods that have been around since G-d created the world. Wrapped up in one oval bundle, eggs contain a yolk, which is rich in fat, protected by the white, made up of protein and lecithin, the latter being a fat emulsifier (a good fat which helps to break down bad fat). I often suggest my clients boost their energy and brain function by starting the day with eggs for breakfast.*

Mock Cheese Latkes

Breakfast, lunch, dinner… Side or main dish… Adult or child… A unanimous satisfied vote of approval!

Ingredients

1	CONTAINER *(8 oz)* TOFU CREAM CHEESE, *softened*
4	LARGE EGGS
4 TBSP	OIL
1 CUP	GLUTEN-FREE OAT FLOUR
4 TBSP	AGAVE, XYLITOL, OR GRANULATED SUGAR
2 TSP	BAKING POWDER
1 TSP	VANILLA EXTRACT
¼ TSP	KOSHER SALT
¼–½ TSP	CINNAMON
•	OIL, *for frying*

Directions

1 In a large bowl, mix together all ingredients.

2 Heat 2 Tbsp oil in a skillet set over medium-high heat. Using an ice cream scoop, measure out and drop batter into hot oil. Fry, turning once, until golden on both sides.

3 Repeat with remaining batter, adding more oil as necessary.

Our *grandmothers said it, our mothers said it, and no doubt we say it to our own children. Breakfast is the most important meal of the day. This particular recipe contains all of the necessary ingredients to start the day off right. It bursts with protein from the cheese and eggs, boasts a wonderful fiber content due to the inclusion of gluten-fee oat flour, and is sweet enough to tempt even the sleepiest child from her bed. The heady aroma that fills your home when you make these might even have your neighbors knocking on your door, willing an invitation to your breakfast table.*

Enjoy these yummy pancakes as they are, or add your own creative touch by sprinkling with shaved chocolate or berries of your choice.

Pancakes

Ingredients

4	LARGE EGGS
¼ CUP	RICE, ALMOND, OR SOY MILK
5 TBSP	AGAVE OR GRANULATED SUGAR
3 TBSP	SELTZER
1 TBSP	OIL
1 TSP	VANILLA EXTRACT
1¼ CUPS	ALMOND FLOUR
¼ TSP	CINNAMON, *optional*
⅛ TSP	SALT, *optional*
•	OIL, *for frying*

Directions

1 In a bowl, mix together eggs, milk, agave, seltzer, oil, and vanilla extract. Stir in almond flour, followed by cinnamon and salt, if using.

2 Heat 2 Tbsp oil in a non-stick skillet set over medium heat.

3 Using a soup ladle or ice cream scoop, depending on the size of pancakes you wish to create, pour batter into skillet.

4 Cook pancakes until bubbles form on surface. Flip pancakes. Cook on second side until slightly golden. Repeat with remaining batter.

This *recipe was born due to repeated requests from clients who wanted a low-carb, high-protein pancake. Almond flour is high in protein and low in carbs. Add eggs to the mix as well as a hint of sweetness and vanilla and you have a satisfying and yummy way to start your day. Remember that if you're using agave, your pancakes will brown quicker than if simply using regular sugar.*

Cheese Blintz Pie

This tantalizing pie makes a statement every time! It's also versatile, complementing many different occasions. Its pretty, sophisticated, scrumptious appearance makes it look more difficult to make than it actually is.

Ingredients

- CREPE RECIPE *(see page 138)*

- BLINTZ FILLING RECIPE *(see page 138)*

Directions

1 Place one crepe on serving plate, pie plate, or platter. Spread a thin layer of filling to cover surface of crepe. Layer with another crepe and then more filling.

2 Repeat layering, using all of the crepes and all except ¼ cup of the filling, depending on how you choose to finish the pie. If you are planning on freezing the pie, end pie with crepe on top and save the filling for garnishing later once the pie is thawed.

Pie Toppings

- Version I: Simply top the pie with the blintz filling, spreading evenly over the top crepe.

- Version II: For a more liquidy topping (which will drip down the sides of the pie), pour a bit of nondairy milk into blintz filling mixture to thin it out. Pour over pie, coating surface evenly.

- Version III: Strawberry Sauce: Puree 2 cups hulled strawberries with ¼ cup agave or granulated sugar. Strawberry Sauce can be used as is or on top of version I or II.

Why *all these options, you ask? Well, for one thing, depending on the occasion, the day of the week, or even the season, sometimes I just feel like one pie over another. For another, I like to have the option of making something visually different. It's so easy to make something pretty. Use the strawberry sauce as suggested above for a burst of color. Serve your pie on your favorite china platter. Pick up a bunch of fresh herbs for that extra special garnish.*

*Simple to make,
yet classy and
delicious!*

Cheesecake

Ingredients

Crust

1½ CUPS	CRUSHED GLUTEN-FREE GRAHAM COOKIES OR OTHER VANILLA COOKIES
½ STICK	*(4 oz)* VEGAN BUTTER OR TRANS-FAT-FREE MARGARINE, *softened*

Cake

2	CONTAINERS *(8 oz each)* TOFU CREAM CHEESE, *softened*
¾ CUP	XYLITOL OR GRANULATED SUGAR
4	LARGE EGGS
2 TBSP	POTATO STARCH
2 TBSP	FRESHLY SQUEEZED LEMON JUICE
•	SPRINKLE CINNAMON, *optional*

Directions

Crust

1 Fill a baking pan halfway with water and place on bottom rack in oven. Arrange the second rack in the middle of the oven for the cheesecake.

2 Preheat oven to 350°.

3 Spray a 9-inch round springform pan or an 8x8-inch square pan with nonstick cooking spray.

4 In a bowl, mix together crushed cookies and butter or margarine until cookies are well moistened. Press into the bottom of springform pan.

Cake

1 In the bowl of an electric mixer, beat together cream cheese, xylitol, eggs, potato starch, lemon juice, and cinnamon, if using, until smooth. Pour mixture over crust. Bake in middle rack of preheated oven for 45 minutes or until sides look done but center still jiggles slightly. Turn oven off. Let cake cool in off oven for 1 hour. Remove from oven; let cool completely in pan on rack.

2 Refrigerate for at least 4 to 6 hours before serving.

This cheesecake freezes beautifully. This recipe also doubles and triples well. Can be used for a two- or three-layer cheesecake.

As *with dairy cheesecakes, it's best not to open the oven the first half-hour of baking. Letting the cake cool gradually, first in a turned-off oven and then at room temperature, helps prevent the cheesecake from cracking and helps to finish the baking process without running the risk of overbaking. Do not place into refrigerator until cooled completely, as it may become soggy.*

Cheesecake & Brownie Squares

Yield *20 to 25 squares*

A superb combination of taste and presentation! I developed this particular brownie, which is not all that sweet, to specifically accompany the rich cheesecake layer. A sweeter brownie, perfect for family gatherings, can be found on page 252.

Ingredients

Brownie Layer

6	LARGE EGGS, *separated*
1¾ CUPS	AGAVE, XYLITOL, OR GRANULATED SUGAR
1½ CUPS	OIL
1 CUP	POTATO STARCH
½ CUP	COCOA POWDER

Cheesecake Layer

4	CONTAINERS *(8 oz each)* TOFU CREAM CHEESE, *softened*
1½ CUPS	XYLITOL OR GRANULATED SUGAR
8	LARGE EGGS
4 TBSP	POTATO STARCH
2 TBSP	FRESHLY SQUEEZED LEMON JUICE

Praline Topping

7 OZ	WHITE CHOCOLATE, *coarsely chopped*
2 TBSP	AGAVE OR GRANULATED SUGAR
8 OZ	BLANCHED ROASTED UNSALTED FILBERTS

Cheesecake or brownie for dessert? Fudgy or cakey brownie? Now you don't have to choose. This spectacular dessert combines both favorites with a brownie that falls right in the middle of the cakey versus fudgy debate. Usually, brownies are a one-bowl wonder. And, although these brownies are not complicated, I found that a few tweaks were in order. Potato starch does not provide the same bounce or foundational structure that wheat flour does. To help the brownies retain their shape, I separated the eggs and then beat them. The beaten eggs provide the support that the potato starch simply doesn't have the strength to do.

Directions

Brownie Layer

1. Preheat oven to 350°. Line a 9x13-inch baking pan with parchment paper.

2. In a large bowl, whip eggs whites until stiff peaks form. In thin stream, gradually add ¾ cup of the agave, mixing until well incorporated. Set aside.

3. In the bowl of an electric mixer, cream together egg yolks and remaining 1 cup agave for 3 minutes. Add oil, potato starch, and cocoa to egg yolks. Using spatula, slowly fold egg yolk mixture into egg whites. Transfer mixture to prepared pan, smoothing top.

4. Bake in center of preheated oven for 1 hour or until toothpick inserted in center of brownie comes out clean. Cool completely on rack. Freeze for 3 hours.

Cheesecake Layer

1. Preheat oven to 350°. Line a 9x13-inch baking pan with parchment paper.

2. In the bowl of an electric mixer, mix all ingredients together until smooth. Transfer mixture to prepared pan, smoothing top.

3. Bake in center of preheated oven for 1 hour, or until surface is slightly golden and firm. Turn oven off. Let cake cool in off oven for 1 hour. Remove from oven; let cool completely in pan on rack. Freeze for several hours.

Praline Topping

1. In a medium saucepan set over low heat, melt chocolate until smooth. Remove from heat; stir in agave or sugar.

2. Place filberts in the bowl of a food processor fitted with the metal "S" blade attachment. Grind filberts on high speed until smooth. Stir filberts into white chocolate mixture until smooth.

Assembly

1. This cake assembles best if the cakes are semi frozen. Cut cakes in half lengthwise. Using a bread knife, cut each cake in half crosswise. Place cheesecake on top of brownie cake. Slice stacked cake into 1½-inch squares.

2. Pour 1 Tbsp of warm praline topping over each cheese squares, allowing praline to drizzle down the sides.

Freezes well for up to 6 months.

Dairy-Free Cheese Snacks

Yield *15 to 20 servings*

This rich and creamy sensation got many wows!

Ingredients

- 4   CONTAINERS *(8 oz each)* TOFU CREAM CHEESE, *softened*
- 1   CONTAINER *(12 oz)* VEGAN SOUR CREAM
- ¼ CUP   FRESHLY SQUEEZED LEMON JUICE
- 2 TBSP   POTATO STARCH
- 1⅓ CUPS   XYLITOL OR GRANULATED SUGAR
- 4   LARGE EGGS
- 2 CUPS   BLUEBERRIES, *optional*

Directions

1. Preheat oven to 350°.

2. In the bowl of an electric mixer, beat all ingredients together, except the blueberries.

3. Filling ramekins (4 oz each) half full, divide mixture evenly among ramekins or thick cupcake holders. For best results, use only those cupcake holders that are double lined with either aluminum or cardboard. You may be able to find aluminum-only cupcake holders, which will also be fine. These varieties work better than the paper-only variety.

4. Add a heaping Tbsp of blueberries. (If not using the blueberries, fill containers ⅘ full.)

5. Bake in center of preheated oven for 30 to 35 minutes or until slightly golden.

   Freezes well for up to 6 months.

I opted to add a splash of lemon juice to this recipe for two different reasons. First, the tanginess helps offset the richness of both the cream cheese and the sour cream. Just as important, however, the acidity from the lemon juice helps firm up the sour cream, creating the proper spoonable consistency.

Vegetables are like

little miracles. A seed or a bulb is planted in dirt and then, with time and a little caring in the form of water and sunshine, it is transformed into a beautiful, colorful food that brings joy and nutrients to our table. This whole process amazes and fascinates me. I marvel at the fact that every day a fresh supply of sunlight beams down on the earth, nourishing that apple, peach, or stalk of celery. The rain too is meted out in ideal quantities, the wind carrying carbon dioxide in perfect measure, coaxing the little seedlings as they grow and mature.

I like to keep this sense of marvel and appreciation alive by not only thanking the Creator for it but making sure that my vegetable side dishes reflect their natural state as much as possible, without adornment or embellishment.

Stellar Side Dishes

Lukshen Kugel

A very simple, tasty lukshen kugel with a distinctive vanilla touch. This is the ideal dish to make ahead and stock in the freezer for upcoming holidays or special occasions. I myself make several in the late summer to have plenty on hand for the New Year.

Ingredients

1 PKG	*(16 oz)* BROWN RICE PASTA *(fettuccini or spaghetti)*
4	LARGE EGGS
⅔ CUP	OIL
1 TSP	KOSHER SALT
1 CUP	XYLITOL OR GRANULATED SUGAR
1–2 TSP	VANILLA EXTRACT

Directions

1 Preheat oven to 375°. Line an 8x10-inch deep pan with parchment paper.

2 Bring a large pot of water set over high heat to just under a boil, just to the point where small bubbles form. Sprinkle in some salt. Break pasta into pot. Cook uncovered, stirring occasionally, for 12 minutes. Drain pasta well; rinse under cold water to stop the cooking process. Drain again; transfer to a bowl.

3 In a separate bowl, whisk together eggs, oil, salt, xylitol, and vanilla. Pour mixture over pasta, stirring to mix well. Pour pasta mixture into prepared pan.

4 Bake in center of preheated oven for 1 hour or until top is slightly golden.

Freezes well for up to 3 months. There's no need to thaw this before rewarming, a bonus for busy weeknights or those occasions when unexpected guests arrive. Simply remove any over-wrapping and cook, covered, in a preheated 350° oven until piping hot, about 60 minutes.

It *took me several attempts to be happy with this lukshen kugel. The challenge was to emulate the texture of a wheat-pasta–based kugel, one that held together well and sliced cleanly. At first I tried adding a little oil to the boiling water to prevent the pasta from sticking together, but I discovered that this wasn't all that necessary. What was necessary was clocking the exact cooking time. Because brown rice pasta swells quickly, I made sure not to overcook it. Nobody enjoys overcooked, flabby pasta. Once that was settled, I played around with the amounts of the other ingredients. Whereas wheat pasta can stand up to a certain amount of oil, brown rice pasta would fall part when mixed with that same amount. I toyed with varying amounts of oil, eggs, and xylitol and finally ended up with this perfect combination.*

Yerushalmi Kugel

It tastes and looks like the authentic one, yet I hope I surprised you by making it nutritious and easy to make—no need to caramelize sugar!

Ingredients

1 PKG	*(16 oz)* BROWN RICE PASTA *(fettuccini, spaghetti, or angel hair)*
5	LARGE EGGS
1 CUP	AGAVE, *preferably dark*
½ CUP	OIL
1 TSP	KOSHER SALT
1 TSP	FRESHLY GROUND BLACK PEPPER

Directions

1 Preheat oven to 375°. Line 2 5x7-inch baking pans with parchment paper.

2 Bring a large pot of water set over high heat to just under a boil, just to the point where small bubbles form. Sprinkle in some salt. Break pasta into pot. Cook uncovered, stirring occasionally, for 12 minutes. Drain pasta well; rinse under cold water to stop the cooking process. Drain again; transfer to bowl.

3 In a separate bowl, whisk together eggs, agave, oil, salt, and pepper. Pour mixture over pasta, mixing well. Divide pasta mixture between prepared baking pans.

4 Bake, uncovered, in center of preheated oven for 1 hour or until slightly golden.

Freezes well for up to 3 months. (See Lukshen Kugel on previous page for re-warming instructions.)

Yerushalmi *kugels are traditionally made with white granulated sugar. The sugar is "cooked" on the stove until it liquefies and achieves a beautiful amber color. This is what gives the kugel its characteristic golden brown look. This step is not necessary for agave, already found in a liquid form. The darker version of agave will resemble the caramelized sugar color, although, if not available, the lighter agave will do in a pinch.*

There *are probably as many versions of yerushalmi kugels out there as there are potato kugels. Nonetheless, I was tickled pink when a native Yerushalmite, after tasting this rendition, proclaimed that it tasted identical to the ones she found at home in Jerusalem.*

Two-Tone Vegetable Kugel

Yield *6 to 8 servings*

It's this simple to serve a nutritious gourmet side dish. The orange of the sweet potato layer contrasts beautifully with the deep green of the broccoli layer.

Ingredients

2	LARGE SWEET POTATOES
1½ LB	FROZEN BROCCOLI FLORETS
2	LARGE EGGS
2–3 Tbsp	*(heaping)* MAYONNAISE, *divided*
2 Tbsp	POTATO STARCH, *divided*
2 TSP	KOSHER SALT, *divided*
⅛ TSP	GARLIC POWDER
⅛ TSP	ONION POWDER

Directions

1 Preheat oven to 350°. Grease or line a 9-inch round or square baking pan or dish.

2 Peel and cut sweet potato into large chunks. Place chunks in a large pot filled with water set over high heat. Bring to boil. Add a pinch of salt. Reduce heat; simmer, covered, for 20 minutes or until potatoes are soft. Drain potatoes; return to pot and mash with a potato masher. Stir in 1 of the eggs, 1 Tbsp of the mayonnaise, 1 Tbsp of the potato starch, and half of the salt, mixing well.

3 In a separate large pot, bring water to a rolling boil. Add a pinch of salt. Add broccoli and cook over high heat, uncovered, for 10 minutes.

4 Drain broccoli; return to the pot and mash with a potato masher. Stir in remaining egg, 1 to 2 heaping tablespoons of mayonnaise, remaining potato starch and salt, and garlic and onion powders, mixing well.

5 Spoon broccoli mixture evenly into bottom of prepared pan, smoothing surface. Top with sweet potato mixture, spreading evenly.

6 Bake in center of preheated oven for 1 hour or until the top is golden.

Freezes well for up to 3 months.

To *create a third tier, boil 1½ lb of chopped cauliflower (fresh or frozen) in lightly salted boiling water. Mash and add 1 egg, 1 heaping Tbsp mayonnaise, a pinch of salt, and onion and garlic powders. Spread on top of broccoli layer. Bake as directed.*

Potato Kugel

"I hope you're including your potato kugel in your cookbook" was an oft-repeated request when people heard that a cookbook was in motion.

Ingredients

5	LARGE EGGS
1 CUP	OIL
2 TBSP	*(heaping)* KOSHER SALT
10	LARGE IDAHO POTATOES *(about 5 lb)*, *peeled and cut in half lengthwise*
1	LARGE ONION, *peeled and cut in half*

Directions

1 Preheat oven to 450°.

2 In a large bowl, whisk together eggs until lightly beaten. Whisk in oil and salt.

3 In a food processor fitted with the blade with tiny holes and working in batches, process potatoes and onion until almost smooth. Transfer potato mixture to bowl, blending well with egg mixture.

4 Pour mixture into a parchment-paper–lined 9x13-inch baking pan.

5 Bake in center of preheated oven for 1 hour or until top is browned. Reduce heat to 350°. Bake for 2 hours.

As *many cookbook authors have remarked, there are umpteen versions of overnight kugels, all of them with different methods and all of them delectable. To give my kugel an overnight effect, bake as directed above. Either refrigerate overnight or proceed directly. Pour 1 cup of seltzer or water directly over kugel. Seltzer will lighten the texture. Cover with parchment and then aluminum foil (or two layers of aluminum foil). Bake in a 350° oven for 3 hours.*

Yield *8 to 10 servings*

Our family's potato torte (pronounced "tortisha"). The perfect solution for family and guests who appreciate good homemade food. An extraordinary dish made from simple ingredients!

Tortia

Ingredients

8	LARGE Idaho POTATOES
5	LARGE EGGS
1 Tbsp	KOSHER SALT
5 Tbsp	OIL

Directions

1 Peel and dice potatoes; place in a large bowl.

2 With a fork, whisk eggs lightly and add to potatoes. Stir in salt, mixing well.

3 Heat oil in a large skillet set over medium heat. Carefully pour potato mixture into skillet. Cover and cook for 30 minutes or until bottom and sides firmly hold together and are well done.

4 Remove skillet from heat; remove cover. Carefully, flip the entire tortia onto a dinner plate that is larger than the skillet being used. You may want to do this over the sink as hot oil may drip out.

5 Slip the entire tortia off the dinner plate back into the skillet, golden side up.

6 Cook over medium heat, uncovered, for 15 to 20 minutes or until a crispy edge is achieved.

Using *Idaho potatoes or a similar high-starch variety is very important to the success of this dish. The starch helps hold the dish together and provides a great mouth feel. New potatoes, on the other hand, will lack the requisite starchiness.*

Paprikash Potatoes

Yield *4 to 6 servings*

This is a classic Hungarian potato dish, much loved and revered through the generations. It's hearty and satisfying. I have somewhat Americanized it by offering the option of slightly sweeter ingredients.

Ingredients

2 Tbsp	OIL
1	LARGE ONION, *peeled and diced*
6	IDAHO POTATOES, *peeled and cubed*
1	SWEET POTATO, *optional, peeled and cubed*
1 Tbsp	KOSHER SALT
1 tsp	PAPRIKA
1 tsp	GARLIC POWDER
¼ tsp	FRESHLY GROUND BLACK PEPPER
1 Tbsp	AGAVE, XYLITOL, OR GRANULATED SUGAR, *optional*

Directions

1   Heat oil in a large pot set over medium-high heat. Add onion and sauté until translucent. Add cubed potatoes and sweet potato, if using. Lower heat slightly; cook, stirring occasionally, for 10 minutes. Stir in spices and agave, if using, to coat potatoes well.

2   Add enough water to pot just to cover potatoes. Reduce heat to medium-low; cook, covered, for 35 minutes. Keeping lid slightly ajar, cook for another 10 minutes until water is mostly evaporated and potatoes are very soft.

Paprika *is made by grinding sweet red pepper pods to a powder. The pods happen to be quite tough, so many grindings are necessary. Paprika can range from quite mild and sweet to mouth-burning hot. Unless otherwise specified in a recipe, you can assume that the paprika called for is sweet.*

Potato Knishes

A multigenerational winner. For adults, the dish presents well, and for kids it tastes great. So sophisticated yet so unbelievably easy to make.

Ingredients

5	LARGE IDAHO POTATOES, *peeled and cubed*
4	LARGE EGGS
2½ TBSP	POTATO STARCH
2½ TBSP	MAYONNAISE
1½ TSP	KOSHER SALT
⅛ TSP	FRESHLY GROUND BLACK PEPPER
3 TBSP	SESAME SEEDS *(approximately)*

Directions

1 Place potatoes in a large pot filled with water set over high heat. Bring to boil. Add a pinch of salt. Reduce heat; simmer, covered, for 25 to 30 minutes or until potatoes are tender. Drain potatoes; return to pot and mash well.

2 Add 3 of the eggs, potato starch, mayonnaise, salt, and pepper and mix very well.

3 Preheat oven to 350°.

4 Using a medium-size ice cream scoop, scoop balls of potato mixture onto a parchment-paper–lined cookie sheet.

5 Lightly whisk remaining egg with 1 Tbsp water to make an egg wash. Brush knishes with egg wash and sprinkle with sesame seeds.

6 Bake, uncovered, in center of preheated oven for 45 minutes or until golden.

Freeze well for up to 3 months.

I've *always shied away from freezing any dishes involving potatoes. That is, until two friends with whom I shared this recipe surprised me by saying that of course it freezes well. Naturally I froze the next batch I made, and lo and behold, the knishes indeed came out of the deep freeze tasting just as scrumptious as before.*

Potato Latkes

A classic tradition at the Festival of Chanukah, yet a treat the whole family will enjoy any time of the year.

Ingredients

3	LARGE EGGS
1 TBSP	KOSHER SALT
1 TSP	GARLIC POWDER
5	LARGE IDAHO POTATOES, *peeled and cut in half lengthwise*
•	OIL, *for frying*

Directions

1 In a large bowl, whisk eggs until lightly beaten. Whisk in salt and garlic powder.

2 In a food processor fitted with the blade with the smallest holes, process the potatoes until almost smooth.

3 Stir potatoes into egg mixture, mixing until well combined.

4 Heat ⅛-inch of oil in a large skillet set over medium heat. In batches and adding more oil as necessary, fry large spoonfuls of latkes, turning once, until golden and crispy.

Variation: *For an added hint of flavor, feel free to add 1 onion, grating it with the potatoes. This also helps prevent the potato from discoloring as quickly.*

Tip: *A little trick I use is to cover my skillet once I add the latke mixture. Then, when I flip them over, I cook them uncovered. This method ensures that the latkes are cooked all the way through and are still slightly crisp on the outside.*

Although *I have called for only regular oil in my latke recipe, I often use half regular oil and half extra-virgin olive oil so that the fruity essence of the olive oil permeates the latkes.*

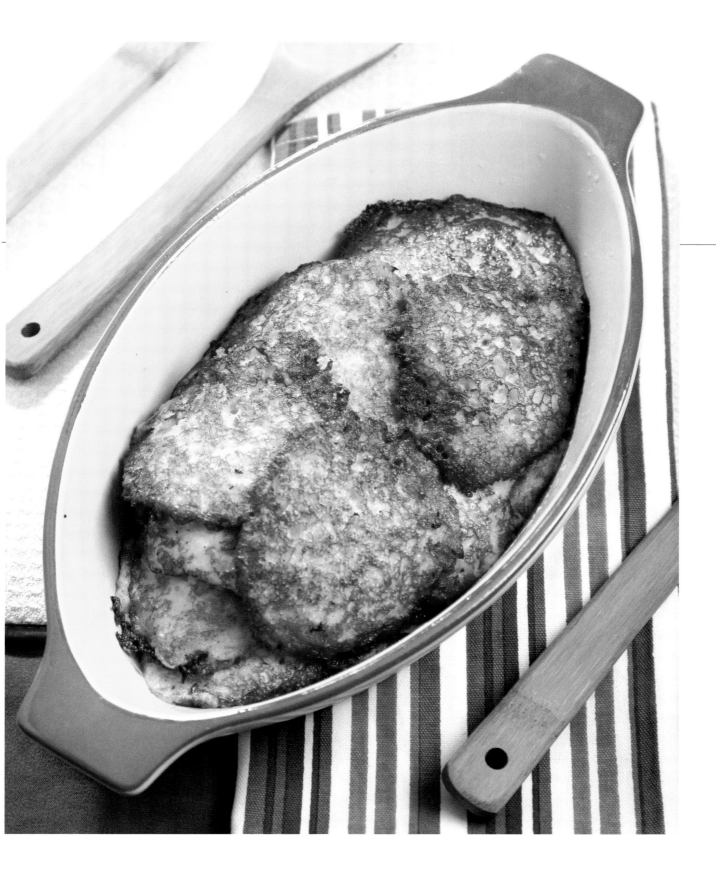

Rosemary Potatoes

Red potatoes are not only more appealing than your typical white, but they also have more fiber. Enjoy them in this quick-to-prepare gourmet dish.

Ingredients

¼ CUP	EXTRA-VIRGIN OLIVE OIL
1 TBSP	DRIED ROSEMARY
1 TSP	KOSHER SALT
½ TSP	GARLIC POWDER
15	SMALL RED POTATOES *(or 2 lb)*, scrubbed, cleaned, and cut in half or wedges

Directions

1 Preheat oven to 425°.

2 In a small bowl, combine oil and spices.

3 Spread potatoes over a parchment-paper–lined baking sheet. Pour oil mixture over potatoes.

4 Roast potatoes in center of preheated oven for 45 minutes or until desired crispiness, tossing potatoes halfway through cooking.

Let *your own sense of flavor dictate which spices you choose for this recipe. If you're a fan of basil, by all means use basil. Or switch it up a bit and add a pinch of both dried cumin and dried coriander. Paprika is also delicious. For a walk on the spicier side, try using crushed fennel or dill seeds.*

Sautéed Vegetables

This vegetable-based dish was incredibly well received by family, friends, and recipe testers.

Ingredients

3 TBSP   OIL

1   LARGE ONION, *thinly sliced in half-circles*

2   CLOVES GARLIC, *sliced*

2   SMALL ZUCCHINI, *thinly sliced*

1   RED PEPPER, *thinly sliced*

1   YELLOW PEPPER, *thinly sliced*

1   GREEN PEPPER, *thinly sliced*

½ TSP   KOSHER SALT

⅛ TSP   FRESHLY GROUND BLACK PEPPER

½ TSP   DRIED OREGANO

Directions

1   Heat oil in a skillet set over medium heat. Add onion and garlic; sauté for about 3 minutes or until translucent.

2   Stir in zucchini, peppers, and spices. Cook, stirring occasionally, for 5 to 7 minutes or until tender crisp.

Fill *out your culinary passport and turn this already wonderful dish into something even more sublime by making ratatouille. This French dish can be achieved by adding 1½ cups of Homemade Tomato Sauce (see page 106) or 1 19-oz can of tomatoes along with the vegetables. Tomatoes contain lycopene, a disease fighting phytochemical, which is much more readily available to our systems when the tomatoes are cooked.*

Peppers *are a rich source of vitamins, minerals, and plant chemicals, making this choice heart and brain healthy.*

Spinach in Shells

This creamy spinach works well not only in shells as described below, but is also equally delicious mixed with a package of spiral pasta or as a solo dish. If making this latter option, be sure to season to taste after combining the spinach with the pasta.

Ingredients

8 OZ	LARGE BROWN-RICE PASTA SHELLS
2 LB	FROZEN SPINACH
2 TBSP	OIL
2 TBSP	OAT FLOUR
1 TBSP	GARLIC POWDER
2	LARGE EGGS
1 TBSP	KOSHER SALT

Directions

1 Bring a large pot of water set over high heat to just under a boil, just to the point where small bubbles form. Sprinkle in some salt. Add shells to water. Cook uncovered, stirring occasionally, for 12 minutes. Drain pasta well; rinse under cold water to stop the cooking process. Drain again; transfer to a bowl.

2 Meanwhile, fill a 6-quart pot half full with water and set over high heat. Bring water to a rapid boil and add spinach. Reduce heat to medium; cook spinach for 5 minutes. Drain spinach.

3 Heat oil in the same 6-quart pot, set over medium heat. Add flour and garlic; cook, stirring constantly, for 2 minutes or until golden brown and a roux is formed.

Stir in spinach until well combined with flour mixture. Stir in eggs and salt, mixing well. Lower heat. Cook, stirring often, for 5 minutes or until creamy and eggs are no longer raw.

5 Place about 2 Tbsp of spinach mixture into each shell. Serve immediately.

Tip: *This spinach mixture freezes well for up to 6 months. Thaw in the refrigerator and then heat thoroughly, uncovered, so it regains its creamy texture.*

Spinach *is one of those unsung heroes of the produce world. It is a rich source of vitamins A, C, and K (which boosts bone density), beta-carotene, and lutein (great for maintaining healthy eyesight), potassium, and magnesium.*

Cabbage & Noodles

Yield *8 to 10 servings*

Both incredibly delicious and highly nutritious, this old-time Hungarian side dish pairs beautifully with fish, chicken, or meat.

Ingredients

½ CUP	OIL
2 LB	SHREDDED GREEN CABBAGE *(or 2 1-lb bags)*
3 TBSP	AGAVE, XYLITOL, OR GRANULATED SUGAR
1 TBSP	KOSHER SALT
½ TSP	FRESHLY GROUND BLACK PEPPER
1 BAG	*(16 oz)* BROWN-RICE SPIRAL OR FETTUCCINI PASTA

Directions

1 Heat oil in a saucepan set over low heat. Add cabbage, agave, salt, and pepper. Cook, stirring occasionally, for about 1 hour or until cabbage is very soft.

2 Meanwhile, bring a large pot of water set over high heat to just under a boil, just to the point where small bubbles form. Sprinkle in some salt. Add pasta to water. Cook uncovered, stirring occasionally, for 12 minutes. Drain pasta well; rinse under cold water to stop the cooking process. Drain again. Add pasta to cabbage, mixing well.

3 Cook for additional 5 minutes or until your dish is piping hot.

The sautéed cabbage freezes very well for up to 4 months. Reheat cabbage in saucepan and simply cook fresh pasta for it. The complete dish will keep fresh for 2 days in the fridge. Make sure the pasta is well coated before refrigerating.

Cabbage *is a member of the cruciferous family which also includes broccoli, bok choy, Brussels sprouts, cauliflower, rapini, and turnip. There are about 5 different kinds of cabbage, but regardless of which variety you buy you can rest easy that cabbage is a good source of calcium and phytochemicals. It's also low in calories and contains vitamin K.*

Coconut String Beans

This uniquely flavored, crispy-crunchy "green" complements any plate.

Ingredients

1 LB	GREEN BEANS, *washed and trimmed*
1 TBSP	FRESHLY SQUEEZED LEMON JUICE
2 TBSP	AGAVE, XYLITOL, OR GRANULATED SUGAR
¼ CUP	DRIED UNSWEETENED SHREDDED COCONUT
•	KOSHER SALT

Directions

1. Fill an 8-quart pot halfway with water. Bring to a rolling boil. Add a pinch of salt.

2. Add green beans, lemon juice, and agave and cook for 5 to 7 minutes, or until beans are crisp and tender.

3. Drain beans. Transfer to serving dish. Sprinkle coconut over beans before serving.

Although *the photo on the facing page features regular shredded coconut, feel free to toast the coconut before sprinkling it over the green beans. Toasted coconut has a lovely golden color and toasting helps round out its flavor. Simply place coconut in a dry skillet set over medium heat. Cook, shaking pan often to redistribute the coconut, for about 5 minutes or until golden brown. For most green vegetables, such as green beans, 7 minutes is the magic number. After 7 minutes of boiling time, string beans will start to lose their vibrant green color, so don't stray too far from the stovetop.*

Zucchini Mushroom Frittata

Yield *8 to 10 servings*

A healthy hit! This tasty combination of eggs, zucchini, and mushrooms is an ideal side dish for any festive occasion.

Ingredients

2 TSP	OIL
1	LARGE ONION, *diced*
4	ZUCCHINI, *diced*
1 TSP	KOSHER SALT
½ TSP	ONION POWDER
½ TSP	GARLIC POWDER
PINCH	FRESHLY GROUND BLACK PEPPER
1 BOX	*(8–10 oz)* FRESH MUSHROOMS *(buttons or stuffers)*
2	LARGE EGGS
2½ TBSP	AGAVE OR GRANULATED SUGAR
2 TBSP	MAYONNAISE

Directions

1 Preheat oven to 350°.

2 Heat oil in a skillet set over medium heat. Add onion; cook until translucent. Reduce heat to medium-low. Stir in zucchini and spices. Cook until softened, without adding any extra water, for about 15 minutes. Zucchini lets off an abundance of its own natural moisture, so no added water is necessary.

3 Meanwhile, peel mushroom caps, if desired. Cut stems off mushrooms; slice thinly. Add mushrooms to skillet. Cook for 10 minutes. Cool slightly. If the mixture is very watery, spill out some liquid. You don't want it to be mushy.

4 In a bowl, beat eggs with a fork. Add agave and mayonnaise. Stir egg mixture into zucchini.

5 Pour mixture into 9-inch round baking pan or glass pie dish.

6 Bake in center of preheated oven for 1 hour or until the top is golden.

Freezes well for up to 3 months. For optimal results, rewarm uncovered.

To *turn this recipe into party-worthy hors d'oeuvres, line individual bite-size foil cups or stainless steel molds with your favorite gluten-free pastry. Fill ¾ full with filling. Bake in a 350° oven for 35 to 40 minutes or until set. For added panache, vary your fillings so your guests will always have a different flavor sensation.*

Sweet Carrots

Caramelization helps sweeten and deepen the flavor of the carrots, which is then highlighted by the addition of honey.

Ingredients

5	CARROTS, *peeled and sliced (about 1 lb)*
5 TBSP	OIL
2 TBSP	AGAVE
⅛ TSP	KOSHER SALT
1 TBSP	HONEY

Directions

1 Place carrots, oil, agave, and salt in a 3-quart saucepan set over low heat. Cook, stirring, for 30 minutes.

2 Add honey and continue cooking uncovered for additional 5 to 10 minutes.

Freezes very well for up to 6 months.

The *humble carrot is one of the most nutritious root vegetables. It is the richest source of beta-carotene, which in fact is what gives it its dark orange color. Beta-carotene is a fat-soluble compound. This means that eating carrots or the like with a little bit of oil actually makes the carotene more accessible to you. Try using a heart-healthy fat such as olive oil.*

Apple Muffins

These muffins can be enjoyed by children as a snack or by adults as a warm side dish, and have the added benefit of being an excellent backup in the freezer, ideal for busy moms.

Ingredients

6	LARGE EGGS
1 CUP	OIL
¾ CUP	AGAVE, XYLITOL, OR GRANULATED SUGAR
1 CUP	TAPIOCA FLOUR
1 CUP	BROWN RICE FLOUR
2 TSP	CINNAMON, *optional*
1 TSP	BAKING POWDER
3	LARGE CORTLAND APPLES, *peeled, cored, and coarsely chopped*

Directions

1   Preheat oven to 350°. Place 24 cardboard cupcake holders on a cookie sheet or line 2 cupcake pans with 24 cupcake papers that are doubled with aluminum foil. Set aside.

2   In a large bowl, using either a handheld mixer or a wooden spoon, mix together the eggs, oil, agave, flours, cinnamon, if using, and baking powder just until a batter is formed.

3   Place 1 Tbsp batter inside prepared cupcake holders; top with 1 Tbsp chopped apples followed by another tablespoonful of batter.

4   Bake in center of preheated oven for 25 minutes or until the top is slightly golden. Let cool in pan on rack.

These muffins can be frozen for up to 3 months. (When freezing gluten-free baked goods, I find that double- or triple-bagging retains freshness.)

No, *your eyes are not deceiving you. There is a recipe very similar to this one in my Cookies and Cakes chapter. The difference is that this one calls for brown rice flour and the other one calls for oat flour and blueberries. I regularly make the above muffins as a side dish, to rave reviews. The addition of blueberries and a different flour somehow kicks it up a notch, making it more filling and less of a side dish.*

Generally speaking,

there are people who bake bread and those who don't. I like to think that anyone and everyone can bake their own bread. This chapter carries the hope that once you try these recipes, you will find how easy, worthwhile, and wonderful baking bread at home can be. If you have bread, you have a meal.

Gluten-free flours are less forgiving than wheat flour is. You have to follow the measurements as if you were making cakes and cookies, at least at the start. Breads made with oat flour and other alternative flours may not rise or double in bulk the way regular bread doughs do. After making a few loaves, you'll be able to tell just by feel if a dough or batter has the right amount of flour

or water in it. Remember that breads should be removed from their pans soon after emerging from the oven in order to prevent them from getting soggy.

One of those indefinable things that affects baking, especially bread, is the amount of humidity on any given day. It's amazing to think that the temperature in your kitchen can affect your bread making, but it's true. If it's raining outside, or just a humid day in June, the flour tends to absorb water or liquid more quickly. If this is the case, you'll need to adjust accordingly, reducing some of the water or adding several tablespoons of flour to achieve the right consistency.

Beautiful Breads

5–7 small challahs or 20–25 small bilkelach

Fluffy Oat Challah

It is often said, "There's nothing like the smell of challah baking in the oven." If taste and health benefits score high, then it's all the more true.

Ingredients

1¾ CUPS	WARM WATER
4 OZ	FRESH YEAST
2 Tbsp	GRANULATED SUGAR *(or 4 Tbsp xylitol)*
4	LARGE EGGS
1 CUP	OIL
1 CUP	RICE, SOY, OR ALMOND MILK
6 CUPS	GLUTEN-FREE OAT FLOUR
1½ Tbsp	XANTHAN GUM
2 TSP	KOSHER SALT

Egg Wash

1	LARGE EGG
2 Tbsp	WATER

Topping

- SESAME OR POPPY SEEDS

Directions

1. In a bowl, combine warm water, fresh yeast, and sugar (or xylitol). Let stand for 10 minutes or until frothy. (If using xylitol, the bubbles will be smaller and the mixture considerably less airy.)

2. Meanwhile, in the bowl of an electric mixer, beat together eggs. Beating the eggs well gives bounce. Slowly, in thin stream, add oil (which adds additional bounce) and then milk substitute. Beat for several minutes. The speed may need to be medium-low vs. medium-high depending on the strength of your mixer.

3. In a separate bowl, stir together oat flour, xanthan gum, and salt. Pour yeast mixture into egg mixture; mix for 1½ minutes. Add 2 to 3 cups of flour to egg mixture; mix well. Beat in remaining flour mixture. Mix dough for 10 minutes on medium-high speed. This mixing is important to success. In fact, it's crucial to achieving a delicious, fluffy challah.

4. Spray or grease 5 to 7 small oblong challah pans or 2 12-cup muffin tins.

5. Spoon mixture into pans until they are about 90% full. This is more of a batter as opposed to a dough.

6. In a small bowl, whisk together egg and water. Brush egg wash over challahs or pat over the challahs evenly with a wet hand. Sprinkle batter with sesame or poppy seeds, if using.

7. Preheat oven to 375°.

8. Allow batter to rise in warm, draft-free area, uncovered, for 15 to 30 minutes if using sugar, or 1 hour if using xylitol.

9 Bake challahs in center of preheated oven for 60 minutes or until golden brown. Bilkelach in muffin tins will only need 40 to 45 minutes.

10 Immediately remove from pans and cool on racks.

Freeze well for up to 2 months. For best results, rewarm challahs when defrosted from freezer for 10 minutes in preheated 350° oven.

"Taking *challah": Because oat flour is expensive and working with it can be tricky, I recommend that people try this smaller recipe the first time they make a gluten-free challah. Then, once they have the hang of it and know what to look and feel for, they can easily double or triple the recipe to "take challah."*

Be *creative: Spoon batter into pans so that they are only ¼ full. Then with a small ice cream scoop, scoop out one ball of batter and place on one side of* pan. *Then scoop out 2 balls, placing them almost side by side in front of the single ball. Repeat until pan is full of balls. This gives the challah a braided look.*

For *those with an oat sensitivity, even a small amount of challah may, especially at the beginning (healing) stages, be a challenge. Substitute rice, tapioca, potato flour, or starch for part of the flour. Make sure your equivalent still allows it to be a Hamotzi challah.*

Dinner Rolls

Yield *10 rolls*

More fiber please… Slice and toast these rolls and you'll wonder if GF people are deprived of bread after all.

Ingredients

⅔ CUP	WARM WATER
1 TBSP	DRY ACTIVE YEAST
3	LARGE EGGS
¼ CUP	OIL
1 CUP	RICE, ALMOND, OR SOY MILK
1 TBSP	AGAVE, XYLITOL, OR GRANULATED SUGAR
2 CUPS	OAT FLOUR
1 CUP	POTATO STARCH
½ CUP	BROWN RICE FLOUR
1 TBSP	XANTHAN GUM
1 TSP	KOSHER SALT

Egg Wash

1	LARGE EGG
2 TBSP	WATER

Toppings

- SESAME SEEDS
- MINCED ONION

Directions

1. Preheat oven to 350°.

2. In a small bowl, combine warm water and yeast.

3. In the bowl of an electric mixer, beat eggs together for 1 minute. Slowly add oil, milk substitute, agave, and yeast mixture. Mix for 2 minutes.

4. In a separate bowl, mix flours and xanthan gum and add to mixture. Continue mixing for 1 to 2 minutes or until well combined.

5. Spray or grease small round roll tins. (Roll tins are a bit wider and shallower than muffin tins.) Scoop batter into roll tins and flatten a bit.

6. In a small bowl, whisk together egg and water; brush onto rolls. Sprinkle with desired toppings.

7. Bake in preheated oven for 35 minutes.

White Rolls Variation

These white rolls scored high! Children consumed their nourishing, high-protein and whole-grain sandwiches in no time with big smiles.

To make these rolls, simply use all the ingredients in the above recipe, but substitute the flours with those itemized below.

Flour

2 CUPS	BROWN RICE FLOUR
1½ CUPS	ALMOND FLOUR
1 TBSP	XANTHAN GUM

Directions

1. Follow directions for the above recipe.

2. Bake in a preheated 350° oven for 40 to 45 minutes or until tops are brown.

Tip: *This recipe doubles and triples easily. 1 egg wash is sufficient for a triple recipe.*

I *slice the rolls once they cool for easy sandwich making. I then freeze them in small sandwich bags. You can defrost them overnight on the counter and then fill them with your choice of egg, tuna, and so on in the morning. No toasting necessary (unless of course you prefer), and it has no GF "aftertaste."*

Wraps with Guacamole

Yield 12 wraps
1½ cups guacamole

The original tortilla wrap is naturally gluten-free and egg-free. I've simulated American-style tortillas with a custom combination of potato starch, tapioca flour, and brown rice flour.

Ingredients

Wraps

2 CUPS	POTATO STARCH
2 CUPS	TAPIOCA FLOUR
½ CUP	BROWN RICE FLOUR
2 TSP	XANTHAN GUM
1¼ TSP	KOSHER SALT
1 TSP	BAKING POWDER
2 TBSP	OIL
2 CUPS	WARM WATER

Guacamole

2	RIPE AVOCADOS, *peeled and diced or mashed*
1	PLUM TOMATO, *diced*
2 TBSP	CHOPPED FRESH CILANTRO LEAVES
2 TBSP	FRESHLY SQUEEZED LIME JUICE (½–1 lime)
½	SMALL JALAPEÑO PEPPER, *diced, optional*
1 TBSP	DICED ONION
⅛ TSP	KOSHER SALT

Tip: *To rewarm wraps, heat frying pan or grill pan over high heat. Place wrap in pan for 30 seconds on each side or until thoroughly warm. Wrap in dish towel until cool.*

You *can try the wraps with or without guacamole. The best method to cook these wraps is by dry roasting, which means to cook in a skillet without oil.*

Directions

Wraps

1. In a large bowl, mix together all the dry ingredients. Form a well in the center of the flour mixture. Pour water and oil into the well; slowly combine by hand to form a dough.

2. Divide dough into 12 balls. If the dough dries up a bit, use wet hands to form the balls.

3. Heat a large frying pan or grill pan over high heat.

4. Roll out one ball of dough between two layers of parchment paper to form a 10-inch circle.

5. Transfer dough to hot pan; cook for 10 seconds. If wraps are left longer, they

will dry out. Flip wrap over and cook for 1 minute or until some bubbles form. You will want to see at least 2 brown spots on the bottom side (take a peak to check), then flip over once again and cook for 1 minute.

6 Wrap in dish towel to cool and to maintain moistness and softness.

Wraps freeze well for up to 2 months.

Guacamole

- In a bowl, mix together ingredients.

Crispy Crakers

The perfect cracker for dips, herring, guacamole, or simply as a snack by itself.

Ingredients

3½ CUPS	POTATO STARCH
6	LARGE EGGS
½ CUP	OIL
½ TSP	KOSHER SALT
2 TBSP	AGAVE, XYLITOL, OR GRANULATED SUGAR
⅛ TSP	GARLIC POWDER
⅛ TSP	ONION POWDER
⅛ TSP	POPPY SEEDS, *optional*

Directions

1. Preheat oven to 350°.

2. In the bowl of an electric mixer, mix together all ingredients until a dough is formed.

3. Divide dough in half. Working with one piece of dough at a time, roll out between layers of parchment paper to $\frac{1}{16}$th of an inch thickness.

4. Remove the top parchment paper; transfer the dough with the parchment paper still under it to a cookie sheet. Repeat with the second piece of dough.

5. Bake in preheated oven for 8 minutes.

6. Remove from oven and cut into 2-inch squares. Rectangles and circles work well too.

7. Bake for an additional 30 minutes or until lightly golden. (Crackers made with agave turn golden quicker than those made with xylitol or sugar.)

8. Allow crackers to cool on baking sheets on rack.

Freeze well for up to 2 months. Crackers will store well in an airtight container at room temperature for up to 2 weeks.

These crackers, like biscotti, require a double bake for a very simple reason. If you cut them into squares before baking, they will grow back together into one seamless sheet of cracker dough. If you wait to cut them until they are fully baked, they tend to crack. However, if you understand their personality and cut them halfway through baking, they will most pleasantly stay in their proposed shape.

Almond Crackers

To those who requested a crispy, tasty cracker that is high in protein, this is for you.

Ingredients

2	LARGE EGGS
2½ TBSP	OIL
¾ CUP	SESAME SEEDS
2 TSP	KOSHER SALT
3 CUPS	ALMOND FLOUR
2 TBSP	POTATO STARCH
1 TBSP	MINCED ONION
1 TBSP	MINCED GARLIC

Directions

1 Preheat oven to 350°.

2 In the bowl of electric mixer, cream together eggs and oil. Change paddle attachment to a dough hook.

3 Add sesame seeds, salt, flour, potato starch, onion, and garlic to bowl; mix well.

4 Divide dough in half. Working with one piece at a time, roll out between layers of parchment paper to $\frac{1}{16}^{th}$ of an inch thickness.

5 Remove the top parchment paper; transfer the dough with the parchment paper still under it to a cookie sheet. Cut into 1x3-inch rectangles. Repeat with the remaining dough.

6 Bake in preheated oven 14 to 16 minutes or until golden.

7 Allow crackers to cool on parchment paper on rack.

Freeze well for up to 2 months. Crackers will store well in an airtight container at room temperature for up to 2 weeks.

Sesame *seeds blend beautifully with almond flour, which has its own subtle nutty flavor. The crispness of these crackers is due in no small part to the ¾ cup of seeds. I also added potato starch, which lent the finishing balance. Instead of minced garlic and minced onion, you can use 2 tsp dried oregano and ½ tsp dried parsley leaves.*

Fruit, like vegetables,

are purely delicious, singularly spectacular, and miraculously perfect in their texture and taste. Their colors radiate their innate and exquisite lusciousness and announce their striking sweetness and alluring essence. Fruit is G-d's dessert.

Indeed, fruit is the ultimate finale. It asks for nothing. Not sugar (well, maybe a little), not a crust (well, perhaps on occasion), and not a topping (mmm, sometimes that would be nice). Okay, I stand semicorrected. Sometimes just a smidgen of dressing up is called for. A crust to house a deliciously melting assortment of apples and blueberries, some rice milk in which to envelop some strawberries and bananas, or some agave to heighten the natural pep of cherries, peaches, and plums. Exuberant and unadorned or slightly enhanced, these fruity finishes fit the bill.

Delightful Desserts

Apple–Blueberry Pie

When I received the comment, "I can't believe that a healthy gluten-free pie can taste so good" from a professional baker, I knew my "tweaking the recipe" days were over.

Ingredients

¾ CUP	TRANS-FAT-FREE MARGARINE, *room temperature* (1½ sticks)
1 CUP	*minus 1 Tbsp* XYLITOL OR GRANULATED SUGAR
3	LARGE EGGS
¾ CUP	POTATO STARCH
½ CUP	BROWN RICE FLOUR
¼ CUP	TAPIOCA STARCH
1½ TSP	BAKING POWDER
¾ TSP	XANTHAN GUM
¼ TSP	VANILLA EXTRACT
3	LARGE CORTLAND OR GOLDEN DELICIOUS APPLES, *peeled, cored, and quartered*
½ CUP	BLUEBERRIES

Glaze

4 TBSP	APRICOT JAM
1 TBSP	WATER

Directions

1. Preheat oven to 350°.

2. In a bowl, combine all of the ingredients except the fruit. Using a wooden spoon, mix well.

3. Grease a 9-inch round fluted tart pan with a removable bottom. Press dough into bottom of pan.

4. Leaving 2-inch circle in the center, arrange overlapping slices of apple in concentric circles, leaving a ⅛-inch border all around the edge so that the dough has room to expand and will create a perfect border. Fill center with blueberries.

5. Bake in center of preheated oven for 1 hour. Cool completely on rack. Remove pie from tart tin.

Glaze

1. In a small saucepan set over low heat, combine jam with water. Cook, stirring, for about 2 minutes or until a loose, liquid consistency is achieved. For best results, press liquid through a fine mesh sieve into a bowl.

2. Brush glaze over apples and blueberries.

Freezes well for 3 months. Thaw in refrigerator.

I love the fact that this dough is so straightforward. It doesn't require a mixer or even a rolling pin. All you need is a large bowl and a wooden spoon, and, of course, a little bit of elbow grease. It's easily pressed into the tart tin with your fingertips and palms. This dough also works beautifully topped with plums or fresh apricots, cut in quarters, skin side up. Be sure to place them together as tightly as possible for optimal effect (no need to leave a border in this case).

Apple-Cherry Compote

Yield *10 to 12 servings*

Apples and cherries both contain soluble fiber, which is helpful for controlling "bad" blood cholesterol levels, among their other high-ranking nutritional properties.

Ingredients

10	LARGE CORTLAND APPLES, *peeled, cored, and cut into wedges*
2½ LB	CHERRIES, *washed and pitted (about 6 cups)*
½ CUP	AGAVE, XYLITOL, OR GRANULATED SUGAR, *optional*

Directions

1 Place apples and cherries in an 8-quart pot and add enough water to cover ¾ of fruit. Stir in sweetener, if using.

2 Bring mixture to a boil. Reduce heat to medium-low; cook, stirring often, for 45 minutes or until apples are soft and a little mushy.

3 Chill before serving.

Freezes well for up to 6 months.

For *this compote, it's important to choose apples that will break down. Cortlands are perfect, but you can also use Macintosh apples. Fruit is full of natural sugars, which are highlighted the more you cook the fruit.*

Baked Apples

This isn't just another baked apple recipe. By adding more fruit than is the norm, I've upped the nutritional and taste ante considerably.

Ingredients

6–8   LARGE CORTLAND APPLES, *washed well*

2 CUPS   PEELED AND DICED MANGO

2 CUPS   BLUEBERRIES, *optional*

•   CINNAMON, *for sprinkling*

Directions

1   Preheat oven to 350°.

2   Cut 1 inch off from top of apples to form a lid. Set aside. Using a soupspoon, core apples, forming an empty cavity.

3   Place apples in a 9x13-inch baking pan lined with parchment paper.

4   Place 2 Tbsp mangoes and blueberries, if using, into empty apple cavities. The fruit will overflow a bit. Sprinkle cinnamon on top of diced mango. Place apple lid on top.

5   Bake, uncovered, for 1 hour or until a bit soft. If you prefer a juicier, softer apple, bake for 1½ hours.

You *may, once you reach the end of this chapter, accuse me of sounding like a broken record, but I really feel that G-d created vibrant, succulent, juicy, and naturally sweet gems that we should take advantage of in all their glory. In other words, why sugarcoat them?*

Purple Applesauce

This recipe's smooth texture and exciting color make it a hit for children (and adults).

Ingredients

10 CORTLAND APPLES, *peeled, cored, and cut into wedges*

7–8 CUPS BLACK SEEDLESS GRAPES *(about 1 large bunch)*

½ CUP AGAVE, XYLITOL, OR GRANULATED SUGAR, *optional*

Directions

1 Place apples and grapes in an 8-quart pot and add water to cover ½ of the fruit. Stir in sweetener, if using. Bring mixture to a boil. Reduce heat to medium-low; cook, stirring often, for 1 hour or until fruit is softened.

2 Using an immersion blender, puree fruit to a smooth consistency.

Freezes well for up to 6 months.

Did *you know that there are over 8,000 different kinds of grapes grown worldwide? Of course, a huge percentage of those go into wine making, and a smaller percentage is dedicated to drying into raisins. Stock your fridge with luscious green, vibrant red, and deep purple grapes for a beautiful canvas. You'll also be getting a cocktail of naturally occurring resveratrol and antioxidants in your fruit tapestry.*

Northern Tropical Blend

In North America we are so blessed with such an abundance of wonderful produce almost all year long that I opted to include peaches in this blend.

Ingredients

5   YELLOW APPLES, *peeled, cored, and cut into wedges*

3   CORTLAND APPLES, *peeled, cored, and cut into wedges*

5   LARGE PEACHES, *cut into small wedges*

1   LARGE PINEAPPLE, *peeled, cored, and diced*

½ CUP   AGAVE, XYLITOL, OR GRANULATED SUGAR, *optional*

Directions

1   Place apples, peaches, and pineapple in an 8-quart pot and add water to cover ¾ of the fruit. Stir in sweetener, if using. Bring mixture to a boil. Reduce heat to medium-low; cook, stirring often, for 20 minutes or until fruit is softened.

2   Chill before serving.

Freezes well for up to 6 months.

Pineapple, *exotic and exquisite as it is, also provides a remarkable menu of benefits. It aids digestion, adds vitamin C to your daily diet and even contains bromelain, an amazing compound that eases inflammatory pain.*

Winter Fruit Salad

Feel the crisp, cool winter breeze as you enjoy this sweet and tart dessert loaded with antioxidants and flavor.

Ingredients

3	GREEN APPLES, *peeled, cored, and diced*
1	YELLOW APPLE, *peeled, cored, and diced (optional)*
3	ORANGES, *peeled, segmented, and diced*
8	KIWIS, *peeled and diced*
1½ CUPS	FRESHLY SQUEEZED ORANGE JUICE
1½ CUPS	SELTZER
2 TBSP	AGAVE, XYLITOL, OR GRANULATED SUGAR, *optional*

Directions

1. Place all ingredients in a bowl and mix well.

2. Chill for several hours in an airtight container or serve immediately.

The *age-old saying that an apple a day keeps the doctor away may not be all that far from the truth. Apples are nutritional powerhouses that often get overlooked. They are a valuable source of pectin, a form of soluble fiber, which can improve the blood lipids profile. They contain vitamin C as well as the flavonoid quercetin, which research has linked to preventing Alzheimer's. Apples should be kept cold so they don't become soft.*

Summer Fruit Soup

I like using ripe, seasonal, succulent summer fruits that are naturally sweeter than candy.

Ingredients

10	PEACHES, *cut in wedges*
7	PLUMS, *cut in wedges*
1 CUP	CHERRIES, *pitted*
¼ CUP	AGAVE, XYLITOL, OR GRANULATED SUGAR, *optional*

Directions

1 Place fruit and agave, if using, in an 8-quart pot and fill pot ¾ full with water. Bring mixture to a boil. Reduce heat to medium; cook, stirring occasionally, for 1 hour. Remove from heat and let cool.

2 Chill for at least 4 hours or overnight. Serve chilled.

Freezes well for up to 6 months.

Fresh *plums are available from late May to around the end of August. Although there are over two thousand varieties grown worldwide, chances are that the eye-appealing fruit you find in your local greengrocer are only from two or three varieties. Plums can range in color from a deep purple to a light rose to a yellow hue. They're actually a distant relative of the peach and nectarine and are rich in phenolic compounds, which promote healthy brain function.*

Lemon Sorbet

Allowing yourself a short-cut or two (a trick every hostess uses) doesn't mean you have to cut back on presentation!

Ingredients

3 CUPS   STORE-BOUGHT LEMON SORBET *(1½ pt)*

2   LARGE MANGOES, *peeled, segmented, and diced (5–6 cups)*

3 CUPS   BLUEBERRIES

Directions

1   Allow sorbet to sit at room temperature for 15 minutes to soften.

2   Transfer sorbet to a bowl and stir until smooth and spreadable.

3   Fill 16 round silicone molds with sorbet. Cover with plastic wrap.

4   Freeze for at least 8 hours or overnight. Unmold 2 molds at a time, placing flat ends together on a dessert platter so they form a ball. Arrange fruit decoratively around sorbet.

Mangos *are an excellent source of vitamin C and a source of beta-carotene. They also contain soothing enzymes which act as a digestive aid. Try to buy mangos that have unblemished yellow skin and a red blush. They should have a sweet fruity perfume and give slightly when pressed.*

Strawberry or Mango Sorbet

Yield *10 servings*

Velvety smooth scoops of sorbet that are healthy, tasty, and homemade can be simple too.

Ingredients

5 CUPS	MANGO SLICES OR STRAWBERRIES *(fresh or frozen)*
2 CUPS	WATER
¾ CUP	AGAVE
1 TBSP	FRESHLY SQUEEZED LEMON JUICE

Directions

1 Puree mangoes or strawberries in blender or food processor fitted with metal "S" blade attachment.

2 Pour mixture into a bowl, then stir in remaining ingredients until well mixed. Cover and refrigerate until completely chilled.

3 Transfer mixture to a 1½ quart (or larger) ice cream maker and freeze according to the manufacturer's instructions.

Here's *an interesting culinary tidbit for you! Sorbet and sherbet are actually not the same thing. Sorbet is an ice made with water, sweetener, fruit or herbs, and sometimes even wine or liqueur. It can be served as a dessert, as it is here, but is also sometimes served as an intermezzo (between the courses) in order to cleanse the palette. Sherbet, on the other hand, is made from water, sweetener, and fruit but contains a dairy product such as milk or cream. It's always served as a dessert or snack.*

Strawberry Banana Ice Cream

I used to believe that store-bought ice cream was always better than homemade. Guess what? Once you become comfortable using an ice cream maker, homemade ice cream can taste absolutely delicious!

Ingredients

½ CUP	AGAVE OR GRANULATED SUGAR
2 TBSP	OIL
6	LARGE RIPE BANANAS
2 CUPS	STRAWBERRIES
1 CUP	RICE, SOY, OR ALMOND MILK
¼ TSP	XANTHAN GUM
¼ TSP	KOSHER SALT

Directions

1 Preheat oven to 400°.

2 In a small plate, mix together 2 Tbsp of the agave with oil.

3 Peel and slice bananas into ¼-inch thick slices. Place slices on parchment-paper–lined baking sheet. Pour agave and oil mixture over banana slices.

4 Bake in center of preheated oven for 30 minutes.

5 Transfer banana slices to blender along with strawberries, milk substitute, xanthan gum, remaining agave, and salt. Blend until smooth. Cover and refrigerate until completely chilled.

6 Transfer to a 1–1½ quart ice cream maker and freeze according to the manufacturer's instructions.

Have *you ever heard of the saying "a rose by any other name would still smell as sweet"? Well, this ice cream is my rose. Although there is no actual cream in it, it is a true delight. You won't even notice the absence of cream. Roasting releases the bananas' sweetness and breaks them down so that they blend well with the other ingredients. This creaminess makes up for the lack of milk fat and produces an ultra-smooth, ultra-creamy ice cream.*

Special Chocolate Mousse

Yield *30 mini dessert cups*

For the meal that deserves that special finale. You'll notice that in the photo we took artistic liberty and adorned the bottom of the glasses with crushed cookie crumbs. This mousse is so rich and sublime that you won't even be aware of the fact that I substantially reduced the amount of sweetener.

Ingredients

3 ROSEMARIE CHOCOLATE BARS *(nondairy praline-filled chocolate)*

12 OZ TRANS-FAT-FREE MARGARINE *(3 sticks)*

6 LARGE EGGS

1 CUP AGAVE OR GRANULATED SUGAR

6 CUPS NONDAIRY VANILLA ICE CREAM *(1½ qt)*

Garnish

• NUT CRUNCH, MINI CHOCOLATE CHIPS, CHOCOLATE SHAVINGS, *optional*

Directions

1 In the top of a double boiler set over simmering, not boiling, water, melt chocolate and margarine together. Transfer to a bowl. Add eggs and agave. Using immersion blender, blend until well combined.

2 Using a plastic cup for flexibility, fill mini trifle or martini cups halfway full with chocolate mixture.

3 Place in a deep pan and cover with aluminum foil.

4 Freeze for at least 4 hours or until firm.

5 Slightly thaw ice cream until malleable. Fill rest of the mini cups with slightly defrosted ice cream. Sprinkle with garnish of your choice. Freeze until served.

This *is a great treat to keep on hand in the freezer for unexpected but special guests. Keep chocolate mousse frozen in a container. Always have some ice cream on hand. Defrost mousse and ice cream for 15 minutes and then assemble. Serve alongside Baked Apples or Apple Cherry Compote, or by itself in larger dessert glasses.*

Apple–Blueberry Oat Muffins

Yield *24 muffins*

Whether you decide to eat these delicious muffins first thing in the morning, as an afternoon snack, or as a tempting finale to your evening meal, they're a terrific way to add more fiber to your diet.

Ingredients

1 CUP	OIL
6	LARGE EGGS
¾ CUP	AGAVE, XYLITOL, OR GRANULATED SUGAR
1 CUP	TAPIOCA FLOUR
¾ CUP	OAT FLOUR
2 TSP	CINNAMON, *optional*
1 TSP	BAKING POWDER
4	LARGE CORTLAND APPLES, *peeled, cored, and coarsely chopped*
1½ CUPS	BLUEBERRIES

Directions

1 Preheat oven to 350°. Place 24 cardboard cupcake holders on a cookie sheet or 24 cupcake papers with aluminum foil in cupcake pans. Set aside.

2 In the bowl of an electric mixer, mix together oil, eggs, agave, flours, cinnamon, if using, and baking powder.

3 Place 1 Tbsp of batter inside prepared cupcake holders; top with 1 Tbsp chopped apples and 1 Tbsp blueberries, followed by another Tbsp of batter.

4 Bake in center of preheated oven for 20 minutes or until tops are golden.

5 Let cool on rack before unmolding.

Muffins can be frozen for up to 4 months.

Blueberries *may be diminutive in size, but boy do they pack a punch when it comes to natural sweetness, taste, health benefits, and beauty. These luscious little berries are laden with powerful antioxidants. They derive their amazing blue tone from a group of phytochemicals called anthocyanins, which help protect against cataract, glaucoma, peptic ulcers, and others ailments.*

Blueberries *are one of the few fruits native to North America. They can range hugely in size. The cultivated variety can be as large as the size of green peas, while the wild genus is usually more akin to small pebbles. Cultivated blueberries tend to be more uniformly sweet, while a hint of tartness characterizes those found in the wild.*

Baking, I'm sure

you've heard, is more of a science than cooking is. After all, you can't throw in a pinch of baking soda like you would be able to with salt or garlic powder and still expect your cookies and cakes to come out beautifully. It's one of the reasons I chose not to include an all-purpose mix of alternative flours in this cookbook. As I developed the recipes for this chapter, I realized that one size, or mix as it happens, did not fit all. I found that my **Chocolate Chip Cookies** required their own customized mix, as did the **Rugelach** or **Shaped Jelly Cookies**. The cakes didn't want to feel left out, so naturally I gave them their unique set of ingredients as well.

Success in gluten-free baking, as in all baking, depends on a couple of things. First and foremost, measuring needs to be accurate. For all of the cakes and cookies in this selection, I used the "dip and sweep" method: I dipped my 1 cup dry measure into the canister of flour until it was slightly overflowing, and then swept the top level with the blunt edge of a knife. This is also how you should measure baking soda or salt, using graduated measuring spoons.

Unless otherwise specified, most of the ingredients called for in baking, including flour, should be at room temperature. Eggs can be removed from the refrigerator 30 minutes before baking to warm up. Remember, however, that eggs separate better when they're cold but will beat up to greater volume if they are then allowed to come to room temperature.

Creative Cakes & Cookies

Chocolate Chip or Pecan Cookies

Yield *25 large or up to 60 small chocolate chip cookies; 30 large or 60–75 small coconut pecan cookies*

"I can't believe it! This is the first chocolate chip cookie that picked me up instead of pulling me down," was a taster's remark.

Ingredients

Chocolate Chip Cookies

5½ CUPS	BLANCHED ALMOND FLOUR
1 TSP	KOSHER SALT
1 TSP	BAKING SODA
4	LARGE EGGS
¾ CUP	OIL
½ CUP	AGAVE OR GRANULATED SUGAR
1 CUP	CHOCOLATE CHIPS *(sugar free if you prefer)*

Tip: *For that added special touch, roast your pecans before adding them to the cookie dough. Preheat oven to 350°. Place oven rack in the center. Spread pecans on a parchment-paper–lined baking sheet. Bake for 10 minutes, mixing once in the middle of roasting.*

Coconut Pecan Cookies

5 CUPS	BLANCHED ALMOND FLOUR
1 TSP	KOSHER SALT
1 TSP	BAKING SODA
4	LARGE EGGS
¾ CUP	OIL
½ CUP	AGAVE OR GRANULATED SUGAR
1½ CUPS	UNSWEETENED SHREDDED COCONUT
½ CUP	CHOPPED PECANS

Directions

For Both Cookies

1. Preheat oven to 350°. Line a baking sheet with parchment paper.

2. In a bowl, mix together almond flour, salt, and baking soda. Set aside.

3. In the bowl of an electric mixer, beat eggs. In thin steady stream, slowly add oil. Gradually pour in agave.

4. Add ½ of the dry ingredients to bowl, mixing until well combined. Add remaining dry ingredients, mixing until well combined.

5. Mix in chocolate chips or coconut and pecans until well combined. The mixture will be a bit firm.

6. Using a medium-sized ice cream scoop, form dome-

shaped cookies; place on prepared baking sheet. Wet the back of the scoop to flatten balls a bit.

7 Bake in center of preheated oven for 13 to 15 minutes or until lightly golden. Remove pan to rack to cool completely.

Variation: *Wet hands to form small balls (the size of a Super Ball) and place on prepared baking sheet. Wet the back of a spoon and flatten a bit. Bake in center of preheated oven for 9 to 10 minutes or until lightly golden.*

It's *fascinating to see how the same recipe made in 2 different sizes can*

have such a different texture. The larger cookies bake to a soft, tender treat. The smaller ones more closely resemble a typical wheat-based cookie, harder on the outside while still soft and chewy on the inside. Feel free to try both, and I'll let you decide which one is more scrumptious. Keep in mind that if you use granulated sugar in place of the agave, the cookies may be a bit crisper.

Oatmeal Chocolate Chip Cookies

Yield *About 18 cookies*

Packed with protein and fiber and sweetened a bit to form a scrumptious oatmeal cookie.

Ingredients

1 CUP	PEANUT BUTTER
¼ CUP	TRANS-FAT-FREE MARGARINE, *room temperature (½ stick)*
¾ CUP	AGAVE
½ CUP	XYLITOL OR GRANULATED SUGAR
2	LARGE EGGS
1¼ TSP	BAKING SODA
3 CUPS	OLD-FASHIONED ROLLED OATS
⅔ CUP	CHOCOLATE CHIPS *(sugar free if you prefer)*

Directions

1 Preheat oven to 350°. Line two baking sheets with parchment paper. Set aside.

2 In an electric mixer, cream together peanut butter, margarine, agave, and xylitol. Add eggs and baking soda. Mix well.

3 Stir in oats and chocolate chips until well combined.

4 Use a tablespoon to drop spoonfuls of dough onto prepared baking sheets. Bake in center of preheated oven for 11 minutes or until golden yet soft. Do not overbake. Remove to rack to cool completely.

Peanuts, *although their name suggests otherwise, are actually not a nut. In fact, peanuts are classified as a legume. I prefer to use kosher organic peanut butter, which is simply ground peanuts without any added hydrogenated fats, sugar, or preservatives. Nowadays, it's not necessary to go organic to get pure peanut butter. Any grocery store will carry it.*

Peanut Chews

Yield *About 4½ dozen rectangles*

These corn-syrup-free bars are simply winners. They're so picture-perfect sweet and peanut buttery that you won't be surprised by the speed at which they're consumed.

Ingredients

1 JAR	*(16 oz)* SMOOTH PEANUT BUTTER
1 CUP	XYLITOL OR GRANULATED SUGAR
1 CUP	AGAVE
7 CUPS	GLUTEN-FREE CRISPY BROWN RICE CEREAL

Glaze

4 OZ	SMOOTH PEANUT BUTTER
14 OZ	DAIRY-FREE WHITE CHOCOLATE, *coarsely chopped*

Directions

1. In a large saucepan set over low heat, cook peanut butter, xylitol, and agave until well blended and xylitol crystals are just about dissolved. Remove from heat.

2. Stir in crisped rice cereal, mixing until well coated.

3. Transfer to a baking sheet, spreading evenly. (This fits perfectly into a nondisposable pan. If you are using a disposable sheet, fill it 80%, leaving a strip of sheet empty so the peanut chews won't be too thin.) Let cool completely.

Glaze

1. In a saucepan set over low heat, melt peanut butter and white chocolate together, stirring until completely smooth. Pour over peanut chews. Let cool completely.

2. Best if refrigerated for at least 2 hours before cutting into desired portions.

   Freezes very well for up to 6 months.

The *texture of these treats depends on the inclusion of both xylitol and agave. The xylitol provides the crispness that is so closely associated with this snack, while the agave lends the requisite amount of chewiness. If agave alone is used, the squares are too chewy. Xylitol on its own results in squares that are too brittle. Hence, a happy marriage was formed.*

Bonbons

Talk about a challenge. I had it in my mind to offer my readers a delicious truffle, but I didn't want to add any cream, a typically essential element. I almost gave up, but then I came up with this rendition and am so pleased that I have it to recommend to you.

Ingredients

4 OZ	SMOOTH PEANUT BUTTER
¼ CUP	VEGAN BUTTER
9 OZ	DARK CHOCOLATE, *coarsely chopped*
7 OZ	DAIRY-FREE WHITE CHOCOLATE, *coarsely chopped*

Coating

8 OZ	DARK CHOCOLATE, *coarsely chopped*
2 OZ	DAIRY-FREE WHITE CHOCOLATE, *coarsely chopped*

Directions

1. In a saucepan set over low heat, melt together peanut butter, butter, and both chocolates. Cool mixture slightly.

2. Refrigerate mixture for 2 hours or until firm enough to form balls.

3. When ready to coat, melt dark chocolate in the top of double boiler set over hot, not boiling water; set aside. Then melt white chocolate the same way; set aside.

4. Scoop peanut-butter/chocolate mixture with a spoon and form balls. Insert toothpick into ball. Submerge into melted dark chocolate, rotating until completely coated. Transfer to parchment-paper–lined baking sheet and remove toothpick. Repeat with remaining balls. Let stand at room temperature for 10 minutes or until chocolate has hardened.

5. Dip tines of fork into white chocolate. Drizzle over coated balls. Let harden.

6. Store in an airtight container at room temperature for up to 7 days.

Freeze very well for up to 6 months.

There *are myriad ways to serve these wonderful little delights. Arrange them on a tiered cake plate, in an antique glass serving platter, or even piled high in martini glasses. Let your own sense of whimsy be your guide. If you're having a large gathering, place two beside your guests' place cards. Or wrap two or three in some cellophane paper or tissue and tie your guests' names to the package. They can also be a lovely hostess gift.*

Rugelach

Mini, medium, or large, this rugelach recipe received the "gold medal award."

Ingredients

2 CUPS	POTATO STARCH
1½ CUPS	TAPIOCA FLOUR
1¼ CUPS	SWEET RICE FLOUR
1 CUP	BROWN RICE FLOUR
5 TSP	XANTHAN GUM
4 TSP	BAKING POWDER
2	LARGE EGGS
2 CUPS	TRANS-FAT-FREE MARGARINE, *room temperature (4 sticks)*
½ CUP	RICE, ALMOND, OR SOY MILK
½ CUP	AGAVE OR GRANULATED SUGAR
•	CONFECTIONERS' SUGAR, *for brushing*

Chocolate Filling

½ CUP	CONFECTIONERS' SUGAR
½ CUP	XYLITOL OR GRANULATED SUGAR
¼ CUP	COCOA POWDER, *sifted*
¼ TSP	CINNAMON

Cinnamon Filling

¼ CUP	CINNAMON
¼ CUP	CONFECTIONERS' SUGAR
1 CUP	XYLITOL OR GRANULATED SUGAR

Directions

1 Preheat oven to 350°.

2 In a bowl, mix together starch, flours, xanthan gum, and baking powder; set aside.

3 In the bowl of an electric mixer, mix together eggs, margarine, milk, and agave for 2 minutes.

4 Add dry ingredients slowly to bowl, mixing well to form a dough, about 5 minutes, adding an additional ¼ cup potato starch if dough is too sticky.

Version I

1 Divide dough in half. Roll out each half until ⅛ inch thick. Invert a dinner plate onto dough; using a small sharp knife, cut around perimeter of dinner plate to create a circle of dough. Remove plate.

Rugelach *come in many different forms, sizes, shapes, and flavors. Tender and soft, flaky and slight crispy, rolled up, sliced, large or miniature. These rugelach, based on an original recipe that contained coffee creamer, fall more into the flaky camp. The agave and milk helps keep them soft, so I've coined a new phrase, "tender flaky rugelach," in their honor. Rugelach will freeze well with or without the sugar.*

2 Place ½ of chosen filling into center of dough. Using the back of a spoon, spread the filling in a circular motion up to ½ inch from ends.

3 Using a knife or pizza wheel, cut dough into 8 wedges, then into 16 wedges and finally into 32. Roll each wedge from the wider ends to the center, jelly-roll style. Transfer rugelach to parchment-paper–lined baking sheet, placing fairly closely together.

4 Bake for 20 to 22 minutes or until lightly golden. Remove pan to rack to cool completely, then sprinkle with confectioners' sugar.

Version II

1 Divide dough into 8 equal-sized pieces. Roll out each piece until ⅛ inch thick. Cut a 7-inch circle out of each piece of dough. (I use a small Corelle soup bowl as a guide.)

2 Place ⅛ of chosen filling into center of dough. Using the back of a spoon, spread the filling in circular motion up to ¼ inch from ends.

3 For a total of 128 rugelach, cut dough into 8 wedges, then again into 16.

4 For a total of 256 rugelach, cut dough once more into 32 wedges. This mini version might be a little difficult to work with.

5 Roll each wedge from the wider ends to the center, jelly-roll style. Transfer rugelach to parchment-paper–lined baking sheet, placing fairly closely together.

6 Bake for 16 to 18 minutes or until lightly golden. Allow rugelach to cool, then sprinkle with confectioners' sugar.

A traditional delight on the festival of Purim. My personal delight was watching several children tasters give me that smile that connotes, "It's yummy!"

Hamentashen

Ingredients

¾ CUP	POTATO STARCH
¾ CUP	BROWN RICE FLOUR
½ CUP	SWEET RICE FLOUR
½ CUP	TAPIOCA FLOUR
1 TBSP	XANTHAN GUM
½ TSP	KOSHER SALT *(do not double when you double the recipe)*
1 CUP	TRANS-FAT-FREE MARGARINE, *room temperature (2 sticks)*
½ CUP	XYLITOL OR GRANULATED SUGAR
1	LARGE EGG
¼ TSP	VANILLA EXTRACT

Filling

1 CUP	APRICOT JAM *(approximately)*

Directions

1 Preheat oven to 350°. Line 2 cookie sheets with parchment paper. Set aside.

2 In a bowl, stir together potato starch, rice and tapioca flours, xanthan gum, and salt.

3 In the bowl of an electric mixer, beat margarine and sugar together for 2 minutes, or until somewhat combined. Add egg and vanilla; mix for 1 minute.

4 Add dry ingredients, mixing until well blended. If the dough is sticky, flour the baking surface and rolling pin with rice flour.

5 Divide dough in half. Roll dough, one piece at a time, between 2 pieces of parchment paper until ¼-inch thick. Use a 2-inch round cookie cutter or glass to form circles.

6 Place ¼–½ tsp apricot jam in the center of each circle.

7 Bring 2 side arcs toward the center, overlapping them on top to form a point. Then bring bottom arc to center, creating a secure pocket of jam. Transfer to prepared baking sheets.

8 Bake in center of preheated oven for 17 to 18 minutes or until tips are slightly golden. Remove pan to rack to cool completely.

Cookies freeze well for up to 4 months.

This *is a great classic cookie dough. It's used below in the jelly or shaped cookies. It freezes beautifully and is handy to have on hand to turn into an afternoon event with your children. It's very easy to work with and is lovely simply baked with multicolored sprinkles on top. You'll notice that this is a recipe where agave is not given as an option. This is because the cookies need to be a touch crispy, so xylitol (or sugar) is the ideal sweetener.*

Shaped Jelly Cookies

Yield *15 jelly cookies or 25 to 35 shaped cookies*

A simple delicious dough, perfect to bake alongside children or for classic Linzer cookies.

Ingredients

¾ CUP	POTATO STARCH
¾ CUP	BROWN RICE FLOUR
½ CUP	SWEET RICE FLOUR
½ CUP	TAPIOCA FLOUR
1 TBSP	XANTHAN GUM
½ TSP	KOSHER SALT
1 CUP	TRANS-FAT-FREE MARGARINE, *room temperature (2 sticks)*
½ CUP	XYLITOL OR GRANULATED SUGAR
1	LARGE EGG
¼ TSP	VANILLA EXTRACT

Filling

¾ CUP	APRICOT JAM *(approximately)*

Directions

1. Preheat oven to 350°. Line two cookie sheets with parchment paper. Set aside.

2. In a bowl, stir together potato starch, rice and tapioca flours, xanthan gum, and salt. Set aside.

3. In the bowl of an electric mixer, beat margarine and sugar together for 2 minutes or until somewhat combined. Add egg and vanilla; mix for 1 minute.

4. Add the dry ingredients, mixing until well blended. If the dough is sticky, flour the baking surface and rolling pin with sweet rice flour.

5. Divide dough in half. Roll dough, one piece at a time, between 2 pieces of parchment paper until ¼-inch thick.

6. Using a 2-inch round cookie cutter or glass to form circles or shaped cookie cutters, form desired shapes. For half of the circle cookies, you may wish to form a smaller circle in the center by using a bottle cap. Transfer to prepared baking sheets.

7. Bake in center of preheated oven for 17 to 18 minutes or until lightly golden. Remove pan to rack to cool completely.

8. Using a knife, spread a thin layer of jam on a flat cookie and place a cookie with a hole on top. Although these cookies taste great fresh, they're even better after 24 hours.

   These cookies freeze well for up to 4 months.

In *many cookie recipes, the instructions call for creaming the fat together with the sugar until "light and fluffy." When you use trans-fat-free margarine and xylitol, the mixture will not become light and fluffy. It's more a question of mixing them until they become "somewhat combined," as I've noted above. This will not detract from the delicious essence of the cookie.*

Chocolate Cake

Yield *7 to 9 servings or 12 cupcakes*

A veritable champion to have in your repertoire! This is the perfect cake with which to celebrate life's special moments. It's a breeze to put together and can do double duty as cupcakes, so why not celebrate every day?

Ingredients

¾ CUP	POTATO STARCH
½ CUP	BROWN RICE FLOUR
½ CUP	SWEET RICE FLOUR
¼ CUP	TAPIOCA FLOUR
1¼ TSP	XANTHAN GUM
5 TBSP	COCOA POWDER, *sifted*
1 TSP	BAKING SODA
1 TSP	BAKING POWDER
2	LARGE EGGS
1 CUP	AGAVE OR GRANULATED SUGAR
¾ CUP	OIL
1¼ CUPS	ORANGE JUICE

Fluffy Filling

1	LARGE EGG WHITE
2 TBSP	AGAVE
⅛ TSP	VANILLA EXTRACT, *optional*

Chocolate Glaze

12 OZ	DARK CHOCOLATE, *coarsely chopped*
¾ CUP	WATER
1½ TBSP	AGAVE OR HONEY
2 TSP	OIL
¼ TSP	COFFEE

Variation: *For cupcakes, pour batter into a muffin tin lined with cupcake papers. Reduce baking time to 25 minutes.*

This *egg white filling is my attempt to replace a whipped cream filling. The egg white does indeed whisk up to a light and airy filling, but it will lose some of this airiness once sandwiched between the two cake layers.*

Directions

1. Preheat oven to 350°.

2. Line bottom of two 7-inch round baking pans with parchment paper circles. Set aside.

3. In a bowl, stir together potato starch, rice and tapioca flours, xanthan gum, cocoa powder, baking soda, and baking powder. Set aside.

4. In the bowl of an electric mixer, beat eggs. In thin steady stream, slowly add agave, then oil, then orange juice. Beat for 2 minutes.

5. Add dry ingredients, mixing until well blended.

6. Divide batter between prepared pans. Bake in center of preheated oven for 40 minutes, or until toothpick inserted in center comes out clean. Remove to racks to cool slightly. Invert cakes onto rack and unmold; cool completely.

Filling and Glaze

1 In a bowl and using a whisk, whisk egg white until foamy. Add agave and vanilla, if using, which will turn the mixture dark. Whisk for 3 minutes or until mixture thickens and turns lighter in color.

2 In a saucepan set over low heat, melt all glaze ingredients together, stirring until smooth. Let cool for 5 minutes.

3 Place 4 large strips of parchment paper around the edges of a serving plate to catch the glaze as it drips. Remove parchment paper from bottom of one cake. Place directly on top of parchment paper strips. Using a spatula, spread filling on surface of cake. Remove parchment paper from bottom of second cake; carefully place

directly on top of filling.

4 Pour glaze over cake, allowing excess to coat sides and pool at bottom of cake. Let glaze solidify at room temperature. Remove parchment paper strips from under cake before serving.

Cake freezes well for up to 4 months, either iced or uniced.

Roll Cake

Yield *12 servings*

This roll cake tastes as extravagant as it looks. The cream recipe makes enough icing for 1½ cakes, so I like to double it and put away two-thirds for use later on.

Ingredients

Cream

1 CUP	TRANS-FAT-FREE MARGARINE, *room temperature (2 sticks)*
7½ OZ	DARK CHOCOLATE, *coarsely chopped*
2	LARGE EGGS
¾ CUP	AGAVE, XYLITOL, OR SUGAR
1 TBSP	COFFEE GRANULES
2⅔ TBSP	WATER *(2 Tbsp + 2 tsp)*

Cake

3 TBSP	POTATO STARCH
2 TBSP	BROWN RICE FLOUR
2 TBSP	SWEET RICE FLOUR
½ TSP	XANTHAN GUM
7	LARGE EGGS, *separated*
6 TBSP	XYLITOL OR GRANULATED SUGAR

Directions

Cream

1. In a saucepan set over low heat, melt margarine and chocolate together.

2. In a bowl using an immersion blender or in the bowl of an electric mixer, beat together eggs, agave, melted chocolate, coffee granules, and water. Cover and refrigerate cream for 2 to 3 hours or until firm enough to spread or for up to 2 days. If you are using agave, you may need to freeze cream for at least 4 hours or overnight to achieve a spreadable consistency.

Cake

1. Preheat oven to 350°. Line a 15x10-inch baking sheet with parchment paper; set aside.

2. In a bowl, stir together potato starch, rice flours, and xanthan gum. Set aside.

3. In the bowl of an electric mixer, beat egg whites until stiff peaks form. Gradually add xylitol. Reduce speed to medium-low. Add egg yolks. Add dry ingredients, mixing until well combined.

4. Pour batter onto prepared baking sheet, spreading evenly.

5. Bake in center of preheated oven for 16 minutes or until well baked and slightly golden. Remove from oven and immediately invert cake onto a clean dish towel. Carefully peel off parchment paper and roll up cake, jelly-roll style.

6. Let cake cool completely, 15 to 20 minutes.

Assembly

1. Gently unroll cooled cake. Using a spatula, spread one-third of cream over entire surface. Roll it back

I skipped the step of sprinkling confectioner's sugar on top of the dish towel before inverting the cake on it. This is a step that you often see called for in rolled cake recipes. It's meant to prevent the cake from clinging to the tea towel, facilitating easy removal. I wanted to develop a cake that didn't require this particular step. The proportions of rice flours and potato starch eliminated the need to coat the dish towel with sugar, which, by the way, contains corn-starch (to prevent the sugar from clumping) and can have a drying effect on the cake.

up, jelly-roll style. Cut off ¼-inch from both ends to trim cake; reserve or eat quietly!

2 Frost surface of cake with another third of cream, freezing remaining third for another use. Chill before serving.

The cream freezes well for up to 6 months. For best results, allow cream to defrost a bit. Mix well by hand or with an immersion blender until well combined. Cream will then be ready for use.

Log Cake

A friend who considers herself a "maven" (being that she loves to prepare and eat non-GF goodies) commented upon tasting this log cake, "GF cakes are really delicious. I would never have believed…"

Ingredients

2	BATCHES CREAM RECIPE *(see page 244)*
8 OZ	DARK CHOCOLATE, *coarsely chopped*
2½ CUPS	ALMOND FLOUR
2 TBSP	POTATO STARCH
1 TBSP	BROWN RICE FLOUR
1 TBSP	SWEET RICE FLOUR
15	LARGE EGGS, *separated*
1 CUP	AGAVE, XYLITOL, OR GRANULATED SUGAR

Directions

1 Preheat oven to 350°. Line a 15x10-inch baking sheet with parchment paper.

2 Melt chocolate in the top of a double boiler set over hot, not boiling, water. In a bowl, mix together almond flour, potato starch, and rice flours. Set aside.

3 In the bowl of an electric mixer, beat the egg whites on high until stiff peaks form. Gradually add agave. Reduce speed to medium-low. Add egg yolks. Add dry ingredients, mixing until well combined.

4 Fold melted chocolate into mixture, mixing until smooth texture is obtained. Pour batter onto prepared baking sheet, spreading evenly.

5 Bake in center of preheated oven for 20 to 23 minutes or until toothpick inserted in center of cake comes out clean. Let cake cool completely on rack.

Assembly

1 Slice cake into 4 rectangles, each 3½ inches wide. Place one rectangle on a serving plate.

2 Using a spatula, spread some of the cream on the surface of 1 rectangle for the first layer. Top with another rectangle, spreading surface with cream. Repeat with remaining 2 rectangles to form a log. Trim edges. Spread remaining cream over sides and surface of log. Sprinkle with chopped nuts if desired. Chill before serving.

When *you beat egg whites for a cake, what you're doing is creating lots of air, which makes for a lighter, fluffier cake. If you're adding ingredients after you've beaten all that air into the egg whites, and invariably you are, you risk collapsing some of that air. The best way to prevent deflation is to add the light ingredients to the egg whites first, in this case the flour mixture. The chocolate mixture, which is heavier, should be added last, and only folded in, since more rigorous action would put the batter at risk.*

Moist Honey Cake

This remains many children's favorite, even though I drastically cut the sugar content.

Ingredients

4	LARGE EGGS
1 CUP	XYLITOL OR GRANULATED SUGAR
¾ CUP	OIL
1 CUP	HONEY
1 TBSP	COFFEE GRANULES
1½ CUPS	BOILING WATER
1 CUP	BROWN RICE FLOUR
¾ CUP	SWEET RICE FLOUR
1¼ CUPS	POTATO STARCH
¾ CUP	TAPIOCA STARCH
2 TSP	XANTHAN GUM
1½ TSP	BAKING SODA
1½ TSP	BAKING POWDER
½ TSP	CINNAMON, *optional*

Directions

1 Preheat oven to 350°. Line a 9x13-inch baking pan with parchment paper.

2 In a bowl of an electric mixer, cream together eggs and sugar. In thin steady stream, slowly add oil, then honey.

3 Dissolve coffee granules in boiling water.

4 In a separate bowl, mix together dry ingredients.

5 Alternating between liquid and dry ingredients, add the coffee mixture and the dry mixture, a bit at a time, until a uniform, smooth batter is obtained.

6 Pour batter into prepared pan, spreading evenly.

7 Bake in center of preheated oven for 1 hour or until toothpick inserted in center of cake comes out clean. Cool completely in pan on rack. Best served next day.

Freezes well for up to 4 months.

A staple in any baker's pantry, baking soda cannot be used without the presence of an acid to activate it. In the recipe above, the naturally occurring acids in the honey serve as the activators. Baking soda also naturally darkens baked goods, so using it in the proper amounts is important. If you're not sure if your baking soda is active, stir ½ teaspoon of soda into ½ cup water mixed with ¼ tsp vinegar. If the mixture bubbles vigorously, your soda is up to snuff.

Nut, Coffee, & Chocolate Squares

The combination of flavors creates a light cake that is rich in taste.

Ingredients

Cake

12	LARGE EGG WHITES
1 CUP	AGAVE, XYLITOL, OR GRANULATED SUGAR
2 CUPS	ALMOND FLOUR
1 CUP	GROUND FILBERTS
2 TBSP	POTATO STARCH

Cream

12	LARGE EGG YOLKS
1¼ CUPS	AGAVE, XYLITOL, OR GRANULATED SUGAR
1 TBSP	COFFEE, *diluted in 1 Tbsp water*
½ TBSP	COCOA POWDER, *sifted*
1½ CUPS	OIL

Garnish

¼ CUP	GROUND FILBERTS

Directions

Cake

1. Preheat oven to 350°. Line 2 15x10-inch baking sheets with parchment paper.

2. In the bowl of an electric mixer, beat egg whites on high until stiff peaks form; gradually add agave. Reduce heat to medium-low. Add the flour, nuts, and potato starch, mixing until well combined.

3. Divide batter between the 2 prepared baking sheets, spreading evenly.

4. Bake 1 baking sheet at a time in center of preheated oven for 30 to 35 minutes, or until toothpick inserted in center of cake comes out clean. Let cake cool completely on rack. Repeat with second baking sheet.

Cream

1. In bowl of an electric mixer, beat yolks. Gradually add agave, coffee, cocoa, and oil. Mix until well combined.

2. Pour mixture into a double boiler set over hot, not boiling, water. Cook, stirring occasionally, for 25 to 30 minutes or until a thick cream is formed. Let cool slightly.

I like to grind my own filberts. First I roast them in a 350° oven on a baking sheet for about 5 to 8 minutes or until lightly golden. I immediately transfer them to a dishtowel and rub them vigorously to remove as much of the outer skins as possible. Into the food processor they go. This is where you have to keep a keen eye on them. All nuts contain natural oils, so if you overprocess them, they can turn into a paste. The best method is to pulse the nuts just until they are finely ground (about 1 minute), and no more.

Assembly

1 Using a spatula, spread half of the cream onto 1 cake.

2 Place second sheet of cake, parchment paper side up, on top of first layer. Carefully remove parchment paper. Spread remaining cream over top of cake. Garnish with ground filberts. Carefully cover with plastic wrap, making sure not to disturb icing. Freeze for about 1 hour or until cake is semifrozen.

3 Slice cake into 2-inch squares. Remove bottom parchment paper and freeze again for 30 minutes before serving.

Freeze well for up to 4 months.

Rich & Healthy Brownies

What do you do when you're repeatedly asked for something sweet and satisfying that is also high in fiber and protein? My response was this brownie, which answers these queries all at once.

Ingredients

1½ CUPS	ALMOND FLOUR
½ CUP	GLUTEN-FREE OAT FLOUR
¼ CUP	COCOA POWDER, *sifted*
1½ TSP	BAKING SODA
½ TSP	KOSHER SALT
2	LARGE EGGS
1 CUP	AGAVE
1 CUP	UNSWEETENED APPLESAUCE
½ CUP	CHOCOLATE CHIPS *(sugar free if you prefer)*

Directions

1 Preheat oven to 350°. Line a deep 10x10-inch baking pan with parchment paper; set aside.

2 In a bowl, stir together almond and oat flours, cocoa, baking soda, and salt. Set aside.

3 In the bowl of an electric mixer, beat eggs. Add agave and applesauce. Whisk for 2 minutes or until well combined.

4 Add dry ingredients and chocolate chips, mixing well until completely blended.

5 Pour batter into prepared pan. Bake in center of preheated oven for 40 minutes or until toothpick inserted in the center comes out clean. Cool in pan on rack.

Freezes well for up to 4 months.

YOU *may very well be asking yourself, "But where is the fat? How can this be a brownie without any butter or fat?" No, my editor didn't forget this ingredient! Not that I mind some fat in my diet, but I purposely omitted it here. The agave and applesauce both lend sweetness and moisture, as does the almond flour. The flour is also what contributes protein to this snack. Fiber comes as a result of the oat flour. Cocoa produces the intense chocolate flavor, while the chocolate chips up the delicious ante all on their own.*

Index